This Stoic Cryptograms Book belongs to:

_____

Carpe Diem Publications

What is a Cryptogram?

A crypogram is a quotation which has been jumbled up.

Your challenge is to crack the code.

Here is an simple example:

LXSQIJPL XCSF VFWJEBAD, PE DPJ PE VFW KPC.
PEEFKXPSB LXSQ SQFEB LQF LXAA NPGB P OBSSBJ
NPC FD VFW. EBCBKP

This is a quote by Seneca.

The hint is 1: B=E i.e. all the B's are E's

Seneca's name is at the end of the quote as he is the source.

EBCBKP = SENECA

Accordingly, E=S, C=N, K=C and P=A.

Armed with this information, you can start to crack the code. Not easy!

Let the intellectual jousting begin!

Here is the answer :

Withdraw into yourself, as far as you can.
Associate with those who will make a better
man of you. Seneca

Carpe Diem Publications

Contents

This book is made up of an easier section and a more challenging section:

SECTION ONE

- 20 quotes followed by the name of the source
- 20 hints - giving one letter away
- 20 solutions

SECTION TWO

- 209 quotes without the source
- 209 hints - giving one letter away
- 209 solutions

GOOD LUCK AND HAPPY CODE CRACKING!

If you enjoy the book, please consider leaving a review on Amazon.

Carpe Diem Publications

1.

LXSQIJPL XCSF VFWJEBAD, PE DPJ PE VFW KPC.

PEEFKXPSB LXSQ SQFEB LQF LXAA NPGB P OBSSBJ

NPC FD VFW. EBCBKP

. . . .

2.

FVML PR FPRIWA? MCFMDR IORPBPGX LVO RMAO

LVPGXR, MGI MCFMDR BOQHRPGX LVO RMAO

LVPGXR. ROGOZM

. . . .

3.

QUDUSOU HSGTYPG DYLDUSG, QUJUVZU HSGTYPG

ZGQPNNJU. KVQDPZ VPQUJSPZ

. . . .

4.

JQM VCFM AM NSEWM JQRDUH CWJHRZM CWF GCDJFCE,

JQM EMHH GCDJFCE AM QSNM. VSFGWH SWFMERWH

. . . .

5.

IVUM BA ZH RIIEH QMVD RVDZWI CGNIH ZH, QMIR

RVDZWI CGNIH GD. TVWUZH VZWIOGZH

. . . .

6.

XEA PACX TDCSAG XR TDMAG UC CUHADLA. WTGLOC

TOGAHUOC

. . . .

7.

N OQDTVDCF AKJO GNLKI N GNC EYZQ AKJOYQ; N

VNQFK YCK GNLKI SDG NC KCKGE. IKCKBN

. . . .

8.

AOD WHBM EDXHJDW FSDF YGAO AOD XHMHV HN GAW

AOHBQOAW. JIVXBW IBVDMGBW

. . . .

9.

YWS PMW IRFQDMXWI, SUQ XO QZRSEF, XDQ XO QZW

AMRSKRABWF PSI SUQRUSF CZRKZ QZWO HUMY

KUSKWMSRSE QZRSEF. WARKQWQDF

. . . .

10.

P AGMRQE WYU RGQT EGU XPFQ P WQUUQC VGCTQ.

TQEQSP

. . . .

11.

CU CH FBU YIYFUH UZTU XCHUEKJ NYBNQY, CU CH

UZYCK DEXOYSYFUH MBFMYKFCFO UZYS. STKMEH

TEKYQCEH

. . . .

12.

THA EY EZ UHY NXSYR HA QSEU YRSY EZ YH VX

TXSAXN, VCY YRX TXSA HT QSEU HA NXSYR.

XQEIYXYCZ

. . . .

13.

HQVLXHE HPVKBPT XU SIXT.   ZPBFKU PKBSTXKU

. . . .

14.

NL QAU SQUYA'J WAQC FNY PNYJZWUY, FU CQA'J

CZAJ JQ OQKKUOJ JFUP. YUAUOZ

. . . .

15.

LAPT FCK UEZFAUS AU PEIIEU VAZF LANZQT,

UEN RNTTBEI VAZF KYCLTNO. TWAPZTZQK

. . . .

16.

MUJTCK XT KCQ BUJTZMUY HD TXLU CM GUXAGQ, HZQ

HD RMXKPXRNU. URXPQUQZT

. . . .

17.

HPT LP APV WAPZ ZOXJX LXUVO UZUFVR HPT; RP

EX JXULH YPJ FV XQXJHZOXJX. RXAXBU

. . . .

18.

TM UGWMONRU ZPUJ GUJMOV NRS VUOPAU ZPUJ

QGCOVMWX. YNOACV NCOMWPCV

. . . .

19.

HUKGK CQ SP SGH YW UKSGCPL SQ FKEE SQ YPK

YW QOKSDCPL. KOCNHKHAQ

. . . .

20.

GHY LOGHRMH XH EJFN WHRHNPG NFGH; JN LPE

JRGE UKPY OL RHMHLLPNE PRV OR SHU UJNVL.

HBOMYHYFL

. . . .

1: B=E	25:
2: M=A	26:
3: G=T	27:
4: C=O	28:
5: H=S	29:
6: C=S	30:
7: N=A	31:
8: H=O	32:
9: Q=T	33:
10: P=A	34:
11: U=T	35:
12: X=E	36:
13: X=I	37:
14: J=T	38:
15: A=I	39:
16: X=I	40:
17: P=O	41:
18: O=R	42:
19: S=A	43:
20: L=S	44:
21:	45:
22:	46:
23:	47:
24:	48:

1.

Withdraw into yourself, as far as you can.

Associate with those who will make a better

man of you. Seneca

2.

What is wisdom? Always desiring the same

things, and always refusing the same

things. Seneca

3.

Receive without conceit, release without

struggle. Marcus Aurelius

4.

The more we value things outside our control,

the less control we have. Marcus Aurelius

5.

Each of us needs what nature gives us, when nature gives it. Marcus Aurelius

6.

The best answer to anger is silence. Marcus Aurelius

7.

A trifling debt makes a man your debtor; a large one makes him an enemy. Seneca

8.

The soul becomes dyed with the color of its thoughts. Marcus Aurelius

9.

Men are disturbed, not by things, but by the principles and notions which they form concerning things. Epictetus

10.

A golden bit does not make a better horse. Seneca

11.

It is not events that disturb people, it is their judgements concerning them. Marcus Aurelius

12.

For it is not death or pain that is to be feared, but the fear of pain or death. Epictetus

13.

Nothing natural is evil. Marcus Aurelius

14.

If one doesn't know his mistakes, he won't

want to correct them. Seneca

15.

Vice has nothing in common with virtue,

nor Freedom with slavery. Epictetus

16.

Reason is not measured by size or height, but

by principle. Epictetus

17.

You do not know where death awaits you; so be ready for it everywhere. Seneca

18.

Be tolerant with others and strict with yourself. Marcus Aurelius

19.

There is an art of hearing as well as one of speaking. Epictetus

20.

Let silence be your general rule; or say only what is necessary and in few words. Epictetus

1.

ZYBGKEC CLYB EBXVMJC SGG CLFIHE CY CLPEMGQ,
EBXVMJC CLPEMGQ CY ZFEKYO.

. . . .

2.

VMD ZISS DP CYIUIHD OYBIHKU UCIVN ZISS PO
VRUIHD PHIU.

. . . .

3.

EDMVD DCF GLK OCZDNO BMRN KU--GLKOPNTA, LO
PLWN LA GLKO ZOLKITNP?

. . . .

4.

QYG ZB MGOID OGJM? YL QYG ZB OD MCHPJL
NZJHPGPB. ZH ZB HYL KYCJCKHLJ HYCH FCULB
HYL MGOIL.

. . . .

5.

Y LWESS QYOA PJDWYPQ UJH VWYXW Y VJKSR IA

ELWEBAR DJ ELT.

. . . .

6.

ZNCCAX LCD DNX VCAD SJXHAHLD, IMD DNX VCAD

MAXPMJ CP SNBAEZEHLA HLO CP PFEXLOA.

. . . .

7.

DF PEN IEZZLR FIEF IL OIA XLFQXRC E BETAX DC

QRVXEFLBQS, ERY IL DC VXEFLBQS OIA YALC RAF.

. . . .

8.

QNPC LEPFGZMXV E YZBNGZL MP ZGLXNZ QNZZLPC PQ

VSZZAO. ,

. . . .

9.

AL DYZ BMQIO-GQZM RZ BZXH, KUXMZ YAW; AL YZ
RZ KDMQIO, KUXMZ SQCMKZVL.

. . . .

10.

PMO AMWGCRCAMOB HWGG YCP LO PMO OYOSE, LFP PMO
POQKMOB, CZ RWYYOBR.

. . . .

11.

KIM JQ QJI BGFFQBI METM C RQGKP NEINU NETYCMV
KIM CM HQ REIYI CM RCKK, SGM JQM RTJPIY MQ
TJP ZYQ.

. . . .

12.

FPBJVIVFPD LBJJ HBYN GI APN HSNUANIA VW
ZJNIIBQHI--WSNNRVX WSVX SNHSNA.

. . . .

13.

NY AYD RXZE JY LB DZBGDV, YM JY LB

IMHXZBN?

. . . .

14.

MR GMT JIUCFDPCRQ GFQWTK JIUCFDPCRQ CMR

SLTGURWAR TV ATW.

. . . .

15.

XJBEQAQZ P FBO LT TRKJE ET GQ LPZQFEQL ET EJPW

QOL BNTOQ--RWQVRNOQWW ET EJQ FTYYROPEC.

. . . .

16.

CU GUUO HSWAUSUGMA, YWM MTUFU ATQWIO YU AQSU

CQFD PG MTUS, MTHM UJUG EFQS MTUS CU SHZ NUM

NQQO.

. . . .

17.

SRD DAE RKKJQDY BFZ RLRQDVJFY TR DPQFRZ

DJIBQZ BHDVFX KJQ DAR GPTSVH XJJZ.

. . . .

18.

XQIV, DAN ADMT RIAL RAIYPOOVD XMVBCQIVC,

YQN RIAL QCVMVCC ADVC.

. . . .

19.

CW XEVI TD STGD, XDSKE VXEDBH LESX CH BCFEX

CW XEVI TD RVX, BDADATDB XESX ADDQRDHH

LSH FCNDR XEDD WVB XECH.

. . . .

20.

ZU RFMGHJU LQ EKTJTNTJ L XZ KXWWU; XGP HKXH

PTWTGPQ FG HKT ZXG, GFH HKT WSXRT.

. . . .

21.

RA SZGG UGTBA CILNQYA TGIYA CIL INRALV VZYV.

. . . .

22.

SI GYXQ BHA VH ZSBK KAXNVED, VI VQ NSAH

ESQ DVTA ZSB UAXFA?

. . . .

23.

QXGONKLBNSC NP ARJRX AGEBR, LAO RPQRFNLBBC

AGS NA FYLXNSC.

. . . .

24.

NVW LEU UIFQ JIOQ EH WESO TVEOU PYHQ, ILB

AIFQ YU DPQITILU HEO EUVQOT, ILB IPTE HEO

WESOTQPH?

. . . .

25.

EB IAJH XP TP EB KAZRVJB VA ES, TRH SMSR

HSTJSJ, XG TRBVDXRY KTR OS.

. . . .

26.

MW LI VLIW VMJ FWOJLUWI LA VMHR MW MHI, HAQ

QJWI AJR SFLWNW PJF VMHR MW MHI AJR.

. . . .

27.

QYDIBIA KU XAYRQIA RAIJRC KI, H KGCR MY

KU MGRU XU QHK RQJR HC JWW RQJR PIIM LYPLIAP

KI.

. . . .

28.

MYEYEPYMZCF DQM PYCYJKNUDML CYYXL CD

UZEY, DM LOZII, DM DBBDMUQCZUA, PQU DCIA

FDDX ZCUYCUZDCL.

. . . .

29.

WK WG JCZ WQFJQGKSQFL, WQ AXPWQQWQP JQX KVWQP SYKXZ SQJKVXZ, KVSK USNXG IWYX GVJZK.

. . . .

30.

WD AR UT ATQMUZD HWV MDXUOR U YATSTDRR HAZWVLZ QANATQ ATZDMDRZ.

. . . .

31.

MHDJWC WLPHLZN JRC VRIHL TB JRC NTWX, PO JCIVRHLF, CUECDHCLVC ILZ CUCDVHNC.

. . . .

32.

XESD JZVHEQ, YUH KMZV XESD JZXX YBQ PEG YFYZUVK KMD VKBEUFDVK OEDV.

. . . .

33.

OXZHKPB PRCZKLBWZ RCAS HMB NRRL RV RHMBWZ,
YCL LBZKWBZ CRHMKCN FXH HR FB RV XZB.

. . . .

34.

KAAY VAWJHTD XC KAAY XTJDTJXATC, KAAY
XURHBCDC, LTY KAAY YDDYC.

. . . .

35.

YQM JQK NZT DM NKLAMWWMC ITKJY TKU QKJ UK COM.

. . . .

36.

XATG DAQGYCQGD UHMQD, ZRY VMCGWODUCB HXIHED
UGXBD.

. . . .

37.

BMNYP XZ HRLQETFLE NY LCALEE QE HTYNEMOLYBE.

. . . .

38.

YKJF IUF VKZXZFRR DSH KIR SCZ REVF IUKZVKZY
SZBW SD IUF HFOFKJFHR KZIFHFRIR.

. . . .

39.

K RLBH PVVW QVYAKXJ, KX GQAVQ HG PVVW
AKBBYHKBTKVA UKHM RSBVOT.

. . . .

40.

CXFRKH AKKNF KS YIYOT HUS UF U DOXYSR, ZVG
DKAAT CXAA SKG YIYS AKKN KS U DOXYSR UF U
HUS.

. . . .

41.

GPZ JITEXGZ JC DSZXCZM BYE GPZ GJVZ, GPZ

TEXGZBNS VXI BYE ZUZE.

. . . .

42.

GH KHR PFOV RCOR SHI COQF ZOBRFG SHIV BRIGS

MP SHI COQF ROINCR SHIVBFEP.

. . . .

43.

MBSLS QX ACYO ACS HUOX HQVVSLSCES NSMZSSC MBS

QCXUCS UCH MBS UCKLO.

. . . .

44.

HM HN FIMMIY MR EJGHNI MXEQ MR YILYREUX.

. . . .

45.

VLFLHD FRP G NGHNGV BLRTH FQ GVKSD BZPM
FSRPQ FQGAPA, BMZIM HL VLP YVLB PMGP PMQD GSQ
ZVCRSZVK RA.

. . . .
46.

PG GPV SJG KW H EGNVC GR XGPVA, DEVHWICV, GC
RHXV, KW HEWG H EGNVC GR XHPLKPT, QIU GPEA JV
SJG KW H EGNVC GR NKCUIV.

. . . .
47.

BZA ZNEZATB YFV ZLPNATB NVAYT YWA GATB
VNTKITTAV NF KLRRLF, YFV GX KLRGNFNFE
UYWNLIT RAFT NVAYT.

. . . .
48.

XU XF Q JXUUJI UEXHB HYU UY CIZDFI PYCL; AIKQHA
XU.

. . . .

49.

IZNCF DTNSZM LNG AP QSCDSPM AF SD, ASG

BNZZNH SD.

. . . .

50.

FWYG LK FLKMJI? YSFYBK GJ FLKW DJZ GWQ KYIQ

GWLURK.

. . . .

51.

XVPCGI IVHVX IVVFC SDV DVAM GR HEGAVIS PIF

XVLJAVCC EWMQACVC GHVX BDELD CDV DPC IG

PQSDGXESO.

. . . .

52.

UTLQXM TA QCM AWEM, VCMQCML ACM TA LMWOCMZ

QCLJXBC IJSA JL BLTMHA.

. . . .

53.

QUETHNQQ UQ B RUHKYBHEN IM IRN PMKW, PAI HMI
IM IRN GUXX, AHXNQQ IRBI WUNXKQ.

. . . .

54.

LQ ALE TQQVT MGXQ UOEGF AHTLQT JEM TE IXWL ME
DQ RGPHTQK DF YEHWQT PT DF LQPGMT.

. . . .

55.

TZ FJVXCI UZ DZAGJZL FSXZNRAFJ DVL NUYZQG
AD GNMADW HNPVLF.

. . . .

56.

CVYI JUVJGU YUUM WZ IDU IBFULZ XVL IDBI
JGUBYOLU EDWPD WY IV SU XVOZH WZ GBSVL.

. . . .

57.

YITYUF WJQJQNJW ODYO AJWU IXOOIJ XF KJJZJZ
VRW IXAXKC Y DYBBU IXVJ.

. . . .

58.

BDQ SZKQ VPH IYHKZUQXK BY SDYV DQ OZLQK,
XPBDQX BDPH SDPB DQ OZLQK.

. . . .

59.

DCY BQTY ISW CST S XAFWDZO BAZDCO AJ CQI,
DCY FWQNYZTY, AFD AJ BCQXC CY XSWWAD MA.

. . . .

60.

XLP ZKJGBPL JMPLKLEPE QJLXS PR ZDIXJV, PNL
TRKPBX PR PNL LPLKMBX.

. . . .

61.

JS CN GZY JZGSNY UJZ FEOSN QZO EGAYJCGM CG
YJCN XCOYKS SHFSDY CYNSVQ.

. . . .

62.

ET YI BULWO, IRIU KTW EATXI QIBW ET JX, PX
EAI XPLU, UTE TK B UTYMI XTJM, YJE TK B
CIBS TUI.

. . . .

63.

FTED ETRYIQ GD RH VH XHHV TEV TDDGDR HRPQID
TEV MHFJUZ NGRP RPQGI NGDPQD.

. . . .

64.

XIGWXMC JYTXJWHTJH ITB BY TYG ZYUS MYU
UHEQGIGWYT, FQG AHG GOWX VISH WGXHAM,
GOYQPO WG FH ZYUXH GOIT ZH BHXHUDH.

. . . .

65.

TERREJ KMHZ ZEWQF PQF ZPTN VWRN ET RHTN--KE HQFWRAN KMN UEFL XWZK ZE GWDM PZ HKZ MNPRKM VNYWHVNZ.

. . . .

66.

RDV EZZ VMW TCW EQY JEVBJNEUVBCQ BQ REJJBQP NSCF CQK RMBZEQVMSCRBU EUVBCQ VC EQCVMKS, VMBQX CN PCY.

. . . .

67.

TG SI EI WARD GDTIMX, SI SBL XAMI HSBP HBL MAP TMPIMXIX; TG SI EI WARD IMINW, HSBP NTUSP SBYI EIIM GADILIIM.

. . . .

68.

JXGOJCV MPS CJWY UHJVSX VPSFCT KH IUHJIHT XSKCR JXT OJDXJXGOSFVCR.

. . . .

69.

QX QUJPGZ JYLNPJ QG JU DGGT QXEGOW HUJ UHOX

WZUQ CURHN MZUHN, VLJ GAGH WZUQ RQYNRHRHN RJ.

. . . .

70.

ML GLHI LXW JINQPALW NZ E SWLSIWMB DPNTP ZPLDZ

E ZLXG IJVLDIV DNMP WIEZLJ.

. . . .

71.

SLN DMIN FGAI ZXE MI DXTNA IX DNKK GI AXS

SX ON OCXQNA OE GAE GRRMPNAS.

. . . .

72.

ABOBW VRXB YI BYIPBW ABNBUURWJ EW

TWEQYIRZCB QEW JEGW NPYCH IE RUX QEW

RAJIPYAS RZMBNICJ.

. . . .

73.

NT MNE IGKPHCLPTF EPNTOF CHOPGT IGKPHCLPTF LKFE
NHF EMX.

. . . .

74.

OT ALJT KEY YTTCJ KXNO, QXG AEYGJ YZGOLYR; GOT
BZZH YTTCJ YZGOLYR, QXG AEYGJ TPTWUGOLYR.

. . . .

75.

NK FONXHIK LH UTNGIOR TNIRK, KH NVO XVOUOXLK
LH KGICWA KHWAK.

. . . .

76.

BLJ GSFJCXNJRR.

. . . .

77.

FM IMOULIP TLOUMWO S DWEDMNY, SIF HYO OUSO SHTSRN CY NMKY DWCHLJ YIF.

. . . .

78.

AZ DEV HVMTVODAIZ IT INM MVLRIZ PAVR LPP DEV ELHHAZVRR IT PATV.

. . . .

79.

GDT CWROT NP FNG KTRFZ CWNVO RA GDT UNAG DSWO GN KTSW.

. . . .

80.

IN FIM QH WMMX DZX FQHN ZNPNE KSDEENJH FQYI DZUTMXU, TSY YEQNH YM ONNC MYINEH MSY MR HYEQRN.

. . . .

81.

PEFNC ONZCTAURA ONFPR   ANZPA.

. . . .

82.

GXZUP GJQ MJZH TB ZG CU RJBZ SPM QUVJZUM

TPXSFGJB.

. . . .

83.

OL XY GWLL KOC EWXYLY EDCQL EFF XPIZWXLY,

EPJ GXPJY EFF OXY ICUY KXROXP OXTYLFG.

. . . .

84.

LIXUHDU AHDM LN HUE, ID ZIN IULDH POTD IULDH

QUFGOFM.

. . . .

85.

XAIWI YAIWI ML NKCYICYDICY YAIWI ML

CK EKRIWYU. MY ML CKY AI XAK AOL FMYYFI, JZY

AI XAK PILMWIL DKWI, YAOY ML EKKW.

. . . .

86.

FDZPY NMAJNT GSQPYM QM DZPAW, PZG QP

MNKAIJTNQGW, HNG QP ONFPGQGW MNJJQXQAPG JZI

FTT DZUAIFGA UAMQIAM.

. . . .

87.

BHQHELH VKYS EA EZ NRJB RVZ MRVHB VESK

QRJBYFH; YZG VKYS EA ZRS, VESK QYJSERZ.

. . . .

88.

HLALE WL BIELVLUU, LALH IWCMP JYIP SU BIVVLF

MHSDQCEPIHP.

. . . .

89.

GU HXQ DXQOP VQPSC VQIROH, CIRCCK LCGRTCB
EFBRGCI LXB EOCFPCBI, MQR RTC JFIC GRICOU.

. . . .

90.

DX RDA BXLXQWT AN DST TSQT ST YEBXYUI YECATW
SQQAFXQW.

. . . .

91.

SMOWCNCH, TMGWJ RGWW NW JLJYH LNYCPJW YPNX.

. . . .

92.

MBPZMTBWSC WJEWSTZ PVB DWQTUWSC XQETBZWSC
QTKXJQZ WS.

. . . .

93.

SDXA KDMR MRH DBIAFDZFE PE MRZN KZNSWEM RPXA MRH ENCAFDZFE SDXA KDMR MRAA.

. . . .

94.

GS GZ TFS HFCQJSP, MLS EFCQSFLZTQZZ, SVXS EXLZQZ ZFJJFU. GS GZ TFS UQXYSV, MLS HVGYFZFHVP, SVXS NGCQZ ZQELJGSP.

. . . .

95.

D ITMVV CMLJ CTJ UQPVZ MI FH KQSWCPH.

. . . .

96.

XWLINRB WE CHR RH LI DKJ ONKRWE; WS EDI LI QHNRD TFZD RH FE, KXX RDWCOE IXEI QWXX DKUI XWRRXI UKXFI.

. . . .

97.

KS KX OFNVWXX SL SJKVR SJFS GW MKI FV WVN SL
YFXXKLVX GJKHJ GW HFVVLS HLVSQLA FS SJWKQ
UWDKVVKVDX.

. . . .

98.

U ME HJ MPYJ; EYOIC YOUXFT YCEPLNI HI XEY.

. . . .

99.

TK WKJ PK DAVS EMYX ZMRWO TRPOXYVMT ZC
IAZQRV KIRWRKW YP ZC JSM JXAJS.

. . . .

100.

DMHQPDC PB BM QMDMSLKAT LB L CSTLH BMXA; KXH
HQLH BMXA PB DMH CSTLH UQPEQ ELD KT BQLYTD KN
TPHQTS OTLS MS CSPTO.

. . . .

101.

KNO KBMO DNCWVHVDNOB, MGWOHH DBOUOGKOY, QCWW
HOBUO KNO HKIKO.

. . . .

102.

QBH UFYHQJ IY TSYH LHEFPLU QBFQ S LI DBFQ
SU XCUQ DSQB EJ DBITH UICT, FPL UFJ DBFQ SU
QGCH.

. . . .

103.

RXQF CES XOJQ OAJOFKQA GON QFESIX DE
NQJQNQFKQ CESNUQBG, CES VOC AHUVHUU OBB
VQFDENU.

. . . .

104.

OJR HVFWOVX HVEEVM JRS RWHIVM HU OJYARQ J
MAQBE CXV WK JII EBJE FWOVX EW LJXX.

. . . .

105.

RKG KGUPKR LJ NTOURF LO USNTOURF UM UW RKG
MLTI.

. . . .

106.

IFTT IBEA PLT IBWTUODLWZ EI PLT YWHJTO QUO PLT
LQPBTO EI PLT VEEO. (

. . . .

107.

DWNWK GBWM LFW MRMHUPUBRM JSD ESPT
WNUGWDPW.

. . . .

108.

RLD YP AFVFW AYSHVUDJ, HVM NHYPL VF MHVCLW FW
ELHW DF HVJFVL.

. . . .

109.

I PILW MNBZO KW ZOIZ ND ZONWT ZOKLEW ICNYZ MOKHO OT KW CYWU.

. . . .

110.

OZSNEOT PZ GKQZJP SLFCLJKOUL EO KRR SNEOTP KP SNL SNZVTNS NZD PNZJS KOX VOULJSKEO REGL EP.

. . . .

111.

LAYM YM FUBDE, LC BSL BOVBHM OYZP LAP MBWP WBD.

. . . .

112.

URWN EWTBVLL NP GV TMWFFVT WQPBF GH NRV TYKYBV UYQQ, MWNRVM NRWB DPQQPU YN!

. . . .

113.

AIB PIZBK BYG XK H MHAZXYHF PMBHANMB ZW
AIB WXPZHF FZKB.

. . . .

114.

ZMHF ZT VTHK ED ARF DR ELWRKFHAF HD MRZ ZT
VTHK EF.

. . . .

115.

BR BQ CLQA RF QLV, LTX CLQAD QRBUU RF JDBRA,
JGLR JA XF TFR ZAAU.

. . . .

116.

YQ CVMJ UYXAXGNN FG JGPMJXGA, PWGJG YN
EOYX YQ YP FG XVP, PWGJG YN XV IVNN.

. . . .

117.

ADMXL OID DI YOIJ BIWS, TMD TSDDSW.

. . . .

118.

CPOF CNDD TA FPA XACOXS QW QLX ZFLSNAZ? FPA

UQTDAZF FPOF GQLDS TA CNZPAS: FPA BUQCDASEA

QW UOFLXA.

. . . .

119.

UW QWA LGOM ASJIMZE MVASMP ASM AJPGQA WP

ASM IZGXM WE GQJ LGQ.

. . . .

120.

LFMP KBMFHWP VUDD HXBUO OHIWPF, JML IBL SPHF

UL.

. . . .

121.

ZKPPKI ZK RKFJYFKR QAI TGBRAI, PUGB PAIPSIKR
JKIJKPSGNNH ZH GPPKOJPF PA RKTKYCK.

. . . .

122.

YODLREI HM EDUYOJ MHBLTOR MHB FRB JYMLD,
EDU LFVDRKM OHL LH EDU MHB LFRW.

. . . .

123.

BYWYSRB DHOOCIMYM OY NH PHWY NVHBY XVH MXYPP
XANV OY.

. . . .

124.

PFUU DEX CER TJOY PFRM DEXY TYERMJY, PME MOA
KEG ZEY MFA OCQJAREY OCG FA EZ DEXY EPC
MJOIJCUD YOQJ?

. . . .

125.

MB MN CONB BH FOOK BIO JOUNBN HJ BIO KOHKYO VMBIHTB BIOMD OEWONNON.

. . . .

126.

Y JERWYZA SALZA ZYK SYLE XYELOKEFH, YKC OKCDVO VRDIA EVOYEWOKE, LJ YK LWXRVEYKE ZRKCLELRK RP FLNOVEH.

. . . .

127.

HCQV XCBD HBDOZIX TQ KBJNDO, EPOO XB WMVZ XCQ FBBZ UDPOMXMQI BN XCBIQ HCB OMAQ HMXC XCQQ.

. . . .

128.

HBCADTX AS VRXN EJ LASHSBNN AN EOI SBVIBNX VFFIEVRT XE XTB HAUASB.

. . . .

129.

OK SOT SVDD MTF ATGRVP JVM HTWWYMPJ VF.

. . . .

130.

AW ERV JUU MIEHRFE XMAS MIF GRYZSMAI, GMSS TAY

M JSMQU, LTRVKT TU HU GSMF AI ZVOZSU.

. . . .

131.

ZN QNL GYWJ YQ XZNE NP TNDB IENLVJC, YQZ TND

RXEE QNL OJ YQKBT YL LVJ LVXJP.

. . . .

132.

LASG JWL J QJK CNL JL LAE OSCL USW LAN

MNKNUDL SU LAN CLJLN.

. . . .

133.

NJIGJIA GJI RWYKI JYR CIXBQI RB CU XBZDPIRG

BA CU VPAXJYRI, GJI QYRGIAR GLGWI LR CYO.

. . . .

134.

FIBK YWCY VCR FZ SCYXDB RWGMW JCHBA KFXD

GSYBDBAY YWB XSGTBDACV, CSO YWB XSGTBDACV FSB

KFX FRS.

. . . .

135.

MD OMT XJL GDZZ MPY NSDJKY MJY JOJCDN; JLN

MD OMT XJZZ GDZZ MPY VJQZGY MJY SDFDLGDN.

. . . .

136.

YAC SQYO JB YAC DAETJWJDACU EW YJ

DUJYCRY, LJY AEW FELC, AEW JET, JU AEW VJSO,

VQY AEW UCNWJL.

. . . .

137.

RAKGK FE ID ASNNFIKEE XAKGK RAKGK FE SIH

YKSG.

. . . .

138.

P XPJJ HVNX ZNI VNX SN CELQ E JNGQ-WNSPNF

XPSVNIS QPSVQD BDIRH ND HWQJJH: PA ZNI XNIJB TQ

JNGQB, JNGQ.

. . . .

139.

RBM KMYR PVXM ZIX WJDMX CY OMNWQ.

. . . .

140.

ETI AKIQNAM RT BKVT XVTPNKZY IK IQTT IQDA

IQT IVZIQ.

. . . .

141.

ITDP VUX TUD CVLD FD? J GJSS QD NJUI VUI

EKJDUISX LT DRDKX TUD.

. . . .

142.

ZSZYDEINJO ILC EQK ILJXTZC, LJX VLJ GZ

VLYYNZX GD KJZ KM EIZF, GHE JKE GD EIZ KEIZY.

. . . .

143.

PFMRAPN AQ HFZS PLMTZLD   MF HLP MRLP BAPKPSQQ.

. . . .

144.

PN WH FWDJNM FPR MRNH GRL OATDLWDN LPTL

DPTHLWLX FPWDP PN ANUEWANH BARK PWH FWBN.

. . . .

145.

RL ATJK ZIEBTLX ITX WNJJMIEJ, EIK FC
JKXNKLQC, FTK FC ANME SIXZL; EIK FC JPMQVK
RITEOJ, FTK FC N OLNOPC ZVNXQL.

. . . .

146.

CRW JENW ZXH SPPYN MTPH REZNWSG XN CRW IECEBWH
XHU NPSUEWO PG CRW MHEQWONW.

. . . .

147.

CPO AMKC HZVVZN VP CZIJ IR SRYMNE VCIR VP
IWZRFZ SV!

. . . .

148.

AREWDH JZQ ESQHAI RA IMH KSNX SV WMRDSASWML;
EJL R ZSI YH IHEWIHQ RZIS WNRQH!

. . . .

149.

XV TRZV FWJR MROJLWVY KRXVO, XUVW XV JUFWH
NWGJUFWQ SLJ IFOJLV QRRC.

. . . .

150.

LJGJW UJ QMLOJLOJY ESOR Z IXHJWTSQSZA
ZHHWJRJLISML MT ZLBORSLC.

. . . .

151.

Y FNYOB YZT EHGB KYZ GLQXPT ZQU WPBB WNQK
PHWB.

. . . .

152.

PBTD NICK QBLVN JIIQ, WIF IJ DMZDWOD BWQ
FKICEVD, ECF IJ JKCRBVLFN BWQ AIN.

. . . .

153.

MI TUN LUNXR XMQC IUF TUNFZCXI, XMQC IUF

UBECFZ.

. . . .

154.

MS TCJ VLRXO PZIFSEBSF DISS DIPT EZFV MLSX MS

CFO QPN DPI XPVLRXQ MLRWL MS WCXXPV AICJ

DPI PASXEJ.

. . . .

155.

TYA YSJ WAJR? YH TYA GHJZNHJ OHSJR.

. . . .

156.

XL MXZ RCOLI AWCRLUNBBT XCI JCVY RXL UVWIR

VSIRCBKLSR ZU XVI YLQR.

. . . .

157.

TU YKO QHHOF MTF YKOFO TD UOTYKOF ISRQV URF DYRFE, MUV DR TU YKO SRXYP DRQS YKOFO TD MSCMPD HOMIO.

. . . .

158.

YKAR, DAPQXCRZC, JKZGE JCBLPA--GCJC LCCD EGC CLLCATC PO ZPPRACLL.

. . . .

159.

CWK EVBTE IGJKL CWGLK PWG NKOC WTA, OBH TL O ZOCWKY OBH NYGCWKY CGPOYH OII AKB.

. . . .

160.

UON GYVN XTR GYEE RLU IHRYVO LAANRSNQV ALQ OYV LGR QNWNRBN, MHU ALQ UONYQ TXNRSXNRU.

. . . .

161.

SVVHLFC LP YLFC ZBVF LJ PVVYP JBV KLCBJ, DNJ

ZBVF LJ LP NFKNHR LJ JMYVP M BMJVSNH FMXV,

MFT DVAUXVP JRKMFJ.

. . . .

162.

KNJQBT H SDPI CJI FUJYO H XOCOPDI, DI VJQBT

ROI XO QCSUHIOPQB CJI IJ UOIQUC DI, HK DP DI

VOUO.

. . . .

163.

MNJX BXW IXJNJF TGXCJYIXJ; SEEGJ CIX

XWJGCAXZ.

. . . .

164.

PXYGUOG BUOK PW UGJ PXGP NO UXWBMK PGFO PXO

ULKO RWP WRMJ WI WBY IYLORKU, DBP WI

. . . .

165.

SWNO QSA XCWNOX SMJMU, UWQSOU QSWJ LOWU, QSOO. DHJVXS QSOR MJCA EVQS EMUTX.

. . . .

166.

Q DIK PIFTEP PB GVCFOG AIJBO, PB DIVP AQPPAG, IVC PB CB PEQVTK LMKGAS.

. . . .

167.

ZML URLFNUA PM XRDM YDMWNRQV LR LFMM LFOU LDQLF.

. . . .

168.

HONSBE NRBHN RML NWLMVZWR UP RML KMFTM FEOS WLBIUAM, AOQM FV FLEP MVTFEKMS OV NFGMWP OV F RBNWOAM AFVS.

. . . .

169.

HQV IPV JQUV VRQE UPP VROV TDEJPHFP YU ONN FQHVOYHPJ YH XEUVYFP.

. . . .

170.

B ERI CRZEPC LEDO MDJ GM SPPFBKAL ZERK LYPRV ZEPG.

. . . .

171.

EY ZNLY B DYBVZBWV, IFBWVNWT SNGU BTBNWIF FDY XBMYI FDBF EYBF BTBNWIF NF JRWFNWKBZZH, BWV JBZUNWT FDY GBTNWT IYB.

. . . .

172.

VRXG OL SAT UQWLSHD, IQ SARS SAD KOLM KRD TFBRLM RLM TFRXS OSITXZ OL SAT ZHTIA ROH RLM ZHTT IGD.

. . . .

173.

XZEVWTK SUH TZV HWNS FZTR UELH UH OK VSJTB;
HSK HKJIKH ZT TZ ZTK OSZ JH TZV NFJTRJTR VZ
SKE.

. . . .
174.

NXUOSVYQ UXW JXR EPUM, LHW RJPW OXQW XI
FYXFTY MXH FTYPOY.

. . . .
175.

UKD TDGB ACNT EUCNSA OS HSONS, QHU UKD ZOAKUV
WDCOEK QV MOERNCM.

. . . .
176.

EH MSB MCAUSHMCFB MVDBH XCIP, KAM DH FCM
DMHBIY MVDBP KO DM, HC DH SB LSC SEH MSB WCLBV
CY QAPXDFX QAHMIO.

. . . .

177.

LO UGAQ COMBF NSBQGO XR GFCOMBFSFY NSKO.

. . . .

178.

DYHFR THTYJER RFB UBHYJJYJHE CD BPYM;

UKR TJHBA UBHYJE OYRF RFYJZYJH RFTR OB TAB

YJWKABL.

. . . .

179.

EFR OQBJ WF KLUIO QRQJ OIOLJ WEFVYEW WEQW UB

WLFVMNOBFTO, FL VXHLUOXKNJ, QXK MO QW

SOQGO QW FXGO.

. . . .

180.

FYGCEY WAZ PXEESXUY, QYYV WAZKYMG VBEY OSWA

XMM WAZ PSUAW.

. . . .

181.

XTEJVK X UZJKHT JH RZJEXIK; RZXJVK PJB

LRKHDC.

....

182.

JDHE MG YZNF VKFHGHTE EDHT EZ XF GZ IFHN EZ

QZPN JMOF HG EZ XF ZT EDMG HSSZPTE IFHNFN EZ

QZPNGFKO?

....

183.

ZS ZI ORZF SD JDHX SJRS OZNSWX PZEE GXIVXFG

ZFSD DWN IDWEI KM VJRFVX.

....

184.

XCFX SCTWC IFXTIPTHI QI TI MHRHB XKK UTXXUH,

FME XCFX SCTWC EKHI MKX TI MHRHB YQWC.

....

185.

ARMQGAK QXKTJFA GL ORLQJLQVJLQ, ARM QXGT

GT B ARMQMJTT EXGOX OBLLRQ NJ QBIJL JBTGFK.

. . . .

186.

LXPH MCJ XCP HVC MDMVCHA AEPP? EP EMH HVCCPL

MDMVCHA EVFHPQK.

. . . .

187.

GUHAU LREX HSS CHBQRBJ, OPE LHK LREX FRAU.

. . . .

188.

WNYOMU FLCCNWHB CU YL HL TLLH YL NXX CUW,

QJUYJUM YJUG SU SLOWH LM ZMUU.

. . . .

189.

SU HSB VCYQUV PSU NYM HQBROV PSU OBBM.

. . . .

190.

MPNBT RN RV BFVRBH NM HBTMLTYB LNNBHQW NOFT

NM BTEMW DMKBHFNBQW.

. . . .

191.

KDXWB XNW DSUWBJI OUHW WGVZXTR PNVX XNW

WBWAUWI PUIN.

. . . .

192.

MEUJSIL QEIDSLUC SC, SIHLCC CWL PC

QEIDSLULF SJJLUHN.

. . . .

193.

YC CYM XIC BYCXQ IZQ CDWZTSOZCYQ, SYF
IMSLOZWN XZQIMQ OC FZQUISLTM OIMR, YMMF
OIZYB IZRQMWK CVOFCYM ZY BZYFYMQQ.

. . . .
194.

KZAFGKC AFSA FSMMJKD GKNHUJD WJ, HKQJDD G
ASBJ GA SD SK JRGQ; SKL GA GD GK WE MZYJU KZA
AZ ASBJ GA DZ.

. . . .
195.

ZY ZW KEWU YA XKKB MEWK SKWZVKW QVAL KOYKVZOP,
MRY FEVS YA SVZGK YFKL ARY.

. . . .
196.

OG VOS MGWLPD L EBYZYGDD JGRLCDG OG OSWGD TSM
LYSNOGM BD CYAMLNGTCX.

. . . .

197.

AUPL PIH GUIDQUIRU AYL QSYMU OSY RPI IUDQSUL
LZFU IYL YXUC QSUDL HUMDLUM.

. . . .

198.

AZBQ MWZUK KBNSP IM DWG OFEM BNZLMUEML SB
UBBYFGO WS SPM SZNSP, AFGVFGO W ZNUM BA UFAM,
WGV BJMKFGO FS RNFMSUK.

. . . .

199.

VN VR OLRN NYDN NYSRL MYS DKL YLXALZ RYSCXZ
JSN HJSM NYLVK OLJLWDBNSK, WSK NYL
RLBKLBQ VJBKLDRLR NYL UVWN.

. . . .

200.

KDUQ VXEJ, CXB FLB VUFP CLLYA.

. . . .

201.

QJ HAUGRT CUW JIYUHJ UGP KJJERJ HUGRH WU QSCJ,
EJFGWM, UP KRFWWJPM.

. . . .

202.

QNF ZRJPFIQ TACQVF AI ZRQ XRIQFCFS JE
AZKFZIF GZS DGCPGZSI, JVQ JE IOFGQ GZS JPRRS.

. . . .

203.

W ZFAGMC DP GETGZQ, YZ HPMM YZ GEIUYQPSGM, WS
W HPUP EAQ IMYC QA FYKP FWJ HFA DPEPSWQZ JP
DPEPSWQ FWJZPMS, YMZA.

. . . .

204.

CDGS HAUH OS EAWLA HAK LAUQULHKQ WJ FUVK
OKHHKQ WJ ICCV.

. . . .

205.

LZ VZE ODPZM AVGYOOYVIOC, ZM
GYEFZAE MWIDML EZ EFW KZHHZV IZZL.

. . . .

206.

YA EYI BTTIGLBCAT GBOXOD ELCY CYA ELGQAM LT IWA
IH CYAX YLXTAOH.

. . . .

207.

BG VBS ADGX OSC TSPG SO VGMTFB MLA YTGMXICG
XBSVX FBMF BG LGPGC BMA M CDNBF FS TDPG.

. . . .

208.

HZC OXXQ FSR DCSTG ESBFBJ FPEZ HZSH NG
RXH CINB, CLECVH HX HZXGC HZSH HSYC NH NBB.

. . . .

209.

OMI BYWA MSB UYHIX OY AEKI TYBO MSUUEAN, EV
BMI HEAA RYO LI SRQEYWB SLYWO HMSO EB
WRETUYXOSRO.

. . . .

210.

HX XHO RT TX MRVM RH UXPNJHO CT HXN NX HOOQ
C UPROHQ CII NMO WXPO, KOFCJTO MO HOOQT
HXNMRHV OITO.

. . . .

211.

EQ EC GEFESAC NEQZNB QS QBACQ VSPSKH SB QS
QBACQ NGNBHPSKH.

. . . .

212.

NBCYGRGNBS LWMXBWR YGZW GA UMI, NEWMXBWR
NWMXW, MIK XMYYR GI LBW PBGYW BTUMI EMXW LG
YCZW CI BMEUGIS.

. . . .

213.

OUSDN KNKZ KVV KBCJWOZ KGDPO VJYW, KBA LD

HKMW JO QVWKLKBO.

. . . .

214.

YD YO UEH OWUHQ TUH RSJD WJQ VX SJI XJOYKA DSJD

BJGXO JKK UEH KYTX IYTTYWEKD.

. . . .

215.

DSNNSO JRS NGPC MRZS RMM.

. . . .

216.

WR WG KYAHVBNOF ZYK POIZ RZV PWAH WG VTIWRVH SU

PYQWAM RZV SYHU.

. . . .

217.

GW EUG E YEXG, WX MEZ WX CW ELZGJDLP DLMDLUNXN WX ILGXIN, YWRRIGNM GJN MWIR.

. . . .

218.

NLY PJ HKMLDMU DZ BPCM PY JZHPMDR LYU GZK DAM HZNNZY OZZU.

. . . .

219.

BGFZTJG TE MWKX PZV WKNG, KEO YTIG MWKXGNGB XTLGR ABTEHR.

. . . .

220.

IRTFCKHOCS AHJCS KN YRJRUXCRJTR VX XFO QRCCXB-ARJ.

. . . .

221.

AOT SLCHUTVA MK TXBPLTV PV AM LRYT MHTV VTYK.

. . . .

222.

VWQ QBX DVOAWD VOPMB, HZ QOVJ, HZ IW DFVWTQ, FT

QBX YZWDWTNW, OD FT QBOQ HG QBW GOQBWZ HG

QBW GOEFVX.

. . . .

223.

OE OR MTRS EQ MS QAEPQLS OL HOLPLSRR.

. . . .

224.

JC LJH KMFWZCK MJC FOZQCNKC KCNQCK UHW.

. . . .

225.

DR RNSQC OAHQ AJ JR SRJNAIQ NR NSQ SVCLRDT
RW NSQ SFLVD CVHQ VJ ADUCVNANFXQ.

. . . .

226.

OFQO RQB LJ BVUVA JQSV EFK HQB XV RKUVZ XC
LBDTAC KA QXTJV.

. . . .

227.

YCVJLYQ GCHVH KCNR VJZY XJZV LH PRQQRW.

. . . .

228.

BFJ IEEK VUK UEMDJ ZVU KEJX UEBFSUI OEC BFJ
XVRJ EO VGGJVCVUNJX, MQB JLJCABFSUI OEC BFJ
XVRJ EO VNBSUI PJDD.

. . . .

229.

YBN GUPN MUF ZC KUYXLN AVKSG XG UMM YZQNYBNL.

. . . .

230.

RTOA BN SZERUABD HWNU GBQ NDKAW DWTLZBGI,

LAHNWA QNZ KGOA QNZWXAIH LAAB SZERAE GD

DKGD NH SZXDTJA.

. . . .

231.

VFJH J DEXBHPU OB FP VFE UJRPB JH FOB

GPAAEV-DPX!

. . . .

232.

D TEIGIQMM MYUOKG PQ WQSOWIQG EI SYQ MDZQ

MCEWES EI VYEXY ES EM PQMSUVQG.

. . . .

233.

FT OP BUPA MGYJRATZMH XFU ZUJYTAP XFRA FRP ITTG YOETG FOB.

. . . .

234.

PF KWNB KWQXSHFK LNFK NIKHX, FN TQVV GH KWM RWPYPRKHY; INY GM KWH KWNBUWKF KWH FNBV QF JMHJ.

. . . .

235.

YIKIWXPS XL HMMHZPNAXPS THZ YHNZIOG.

. . . .

236.

YBTGT NJ C QCYXGCA WTAAMIJBNS CZMQE ZTQ, CQL NY MXEBY NQ TUTGR ICR YM VT SGTJTGUTL.

. . . .

237.

BABFR CHMEB LD DMKB KIF ULN PUI XPBHHD PLZU SQDZLEB.

. . . .

238.

DMWI CX IMH JCYXI AKXCSHXX BJ MCO DMB XHHGX DCXZBO? IB EWXI WDWN XHTJ-EBSEHCI.

. . . .

239.

FURF URCWN XBF FUD APFPEDX LUPAU VBDN XBF URCW FUD NFRFD.

. . . .

240.

BT TBL PMRILZ CJCH IRAL, WBDRO RB RDZ QOCAL SL CAALQDZ JRZPTG.

. . . .

241.

XG GXV JU ICYDVABR AGC ZTYD TV TYU VPDGCDVK.

ZV AJXK SYXQ JXICYDVU, YXK ZV SYMV SGCV.

. . . .

242.

RDAQ YO RAYO AUO QDA JR RJFC, JU KWUMOP,

KJRMPWFOK, KIJUM, SLN ION DWEEI. RDAQ DJY,

HAP J VAUM NA ROO W RNAJF!

. . . .

243.

KNBVOM NC VJM YLQW VJNLZ EJNIJ HYMC LYV IJGLZM,

CY GC VY TM CYPMVNPMC ZYYH GLH CYPMVNPMC TGH.

. . . .

244.

ZUASZ IAH LUSZAUHSMMO, PANSRDA ZWAO SUA

AHKYBAK BXZW UASDYH.

. . . .

245.

RD EVUU KADPK KRDG PB KRD HZLKZA HZDB RVB

NPKVDCKB; PCH ERPK NRMBVLVPC VB PCOAM EVKR

P GPCVPL?

. . . .

246.

WPE TATW EIT OIPMOTCE QBMTWVCIMN MC QBTT

QBPD NKCCMPWC RIMOI DKX PATBCIKVPR KWV VMCEFBY

EIX CTWCT PQ HFCEMOT.

. . . .

247.

ZHQTSZUEZ FRVGL KFQLZ MFQG CK HZROL KQ HQIZ

CKLZHB RUO UQK CKL LSJAZEKL.

. . . .

248.

PZTGBGQYH ZHGQZEL BEGHEGBXE AXZ

BEGHEGBXE, TL SHOO TL TFG AXZ TFG.

. . . .

249.

W PASD ZVLLZA XWU OWLVOYD BHS

UAXAOOVLVAO, IHL UBLQVUR BHS FAOVSAO.

. . . .

250.

VT JVF ZFXME WF JTBA MFZY BXY UHAUZT OE

UFFA, XFW PN RFAWHXTE RBHZW, PHW PN VOE FJX.

. . . .

251.

JYVH FEKASFW, IBK KAVK KAZ LSFG NAEBTG KBHF

KE NELYKASFW BFOEHKAZ EJ V KASFCYH VFG V

RSKSMYF.

. . . .

252.

FK KFJ WH IKSJ SJTZB MK MSJTZ KMCJSH GFZJS CWH

NJJM MCTF CJ QCK CTH AJPKIJ GHJZ MK MTVWFD

WFHGUMH.

. . . .

253.

KQ JKW BVSQU WLBKD DW MWHBQD VD VGGQTVXDQFE,
OLD KQ JKW HQAQVSQU IQSQH.

. . . .

254.

UX TYK ZOYYGV SY FVVB TYKM PURR UL ODMNYLT
PUSO LDSKMV TYK DMV GDXV DLQ XMVV XMYN
ZDMV.

. . . .

255.

QIYEOI RI YEOL P YOJIMKNBJA RI NBEDZK
HOJCJHJVI, QDC PYCIO YEOLJMS JC RI NBEDZK
EMZT CODNC.

. . . .

256.

WGNE OW OAV IRHE IVNWGPH OAV MLVHVGO.

. . . .

257.

MVP QZMX XPZRP BTDP, EJM KTXAFU ZJBPX TM.

. . . .

258.

ESX LPIM ESJE PT VAXX VAUL WJTTPUI PT J

RJTEZX, JIM LJI SJT IUIX LUAX TEAUID.

. . . .

259.

WX RWG MGYYGRE SMCXL QYXSEVLX RZYY FGC TXXQ

WZKEXYM MLGK ZFHVECZIX.

. . . .

260.

GF GU YHFFHT FZ BTZN YTCWHT FOCE XZTH

AHCTEHR, YLF EHGFOHT MCE YH RZEH NGFOZLF FOH

ZFOHT.

. . . .

261.

YG DFUYDZLE HKUY LE LYU CFRLEELER, YALEM ZCGKY
LYU FEB.

. . . .

262.

UAE UXQGPW ODUAYB XG WDG SUUB UI WDG OWFWG FKB
UI WDG PULLAKCWT.

. . . .

263.

DB KBTOFD L SPJNJFMM QTBCFM DELD ZF ELCF
JFCFT SFQD PD PJ BVT DEBVOEDM, BT YFLJD DB
GF OTLDFKVA.

. . . .

264.

JX YJB CPNXG YJXS JX PG OGHXU JOG YOPIXU IBB
ABSC.

. . . .

265.

DCY PZTS DONTW YLYNJ HGWDKXFY ZTDH KT KZS.

. . . .

266.

IDEIMTICPI AHN BHROAB UI CSB BS HNF HGLTPI VAIC

T AHLI UHGI RE UZ UTCG VAHB BS GS.

. . . .

267.

KQPY KHRJU S QPTM UMPYQ CSVU BM UHSVW?

LHBMYQSVW GMVMTHJMVY, ERGJSN-LESASYMU, PVU

VHGJM.

. . . .

268.

QX YXTPJX ZCRRF YF SPM SXXBASL ZCRRASXVV.

. . . .

269.

OPQPMO UG D TDLC VDM PL MCPUBCI MGTNC MGI OCMCIGXL.

. . . .

270.

YS QVZTZ IZTZ TZNWBU SBT XZKYUUYUK QB XZ NUKTA, QVZTZ IBOGE XZ UBUZ SBT ZHZT JZNWYUK QB XZ.

. . . .

271.

WP FRPHIB SG IPBSRLF, ELI NGLBGHPB WRXBPHT ZF CLGDRLK SWES WP RB NEQQRPI EHGLK DRSW SWP MLRJPQBP.

. . . .

272.

DX QPRR WX BH DPK LNOFG OLOPHKY DPK OHLXF QDB NHGXFKYOHGK YDOY PY WXLPHK WC PHVNFPHL DPU MPFKY BM ORR.

. . . .

273.

DWEH FAYH HWG YQAI QM HWG ELNBP FEL XG, DWGL WSY MEVG SY YQ WSJGQAY?

. . . .

274.

WCYKSWI SD DC LFSWNXG FD GCWI DXDLRWDR. JKFY VCX FTT YC YKR TRGFV VCX YFOR NZCH YKR IZFYSYXTR.

. . . .

275.

BGAGRC YGINR VDQK FYFC TDZ WLGWKLMC MG FNN UGXKLZ, FZ KQKLCAGRC VDQKZ FYFC TDZ NDEK.

. . . .

276.

CGOGOHGC MKYM MP EKYATG MKL OVAR, YAR XPSSPI KVO IKP UGMU MKGG CVTKM, RPGU APM SGUUGA MKL VARGNGARGAEG.

. . . .

277.

WU TUD XS ZYAZRSW UB XSKTP ASGLSW, BUV DAUI RIYD WU DAQ WIDQ GKES Z YUGWKSV YDUVRKTP Z FZGG.

. . . .

278.

QP VT YTQA VLDJ SJLHFATW, PZ DJT BJLHZPZBJTA VLHH YTQA VLDJ TNTAUYZFU.

. . . .

279.

IT TIC QGEE CDCL XCLFNJPC HC KWJK G ETDC HZ VLGCIPF KTT HNMW.

. . . .

280.

CKJGIC GRIMOG AK GU XKRB LZGO ZMSUBRSG HKUHWK, RSV GOUCK LOU ARQK IH GOKZB AZSVC LZGOUIG KJRAZSRGZUS.

. . . .

281.

XSVZC XEDCGFN PSCZ CZSFN EPF PNUKEFI, XED IZN
PSBB VSJN CZNN FEFN PZSLZ LUF TN GINO
UVUSFIC ZNDINBX.

. . . .
282.

BP PBQ ULB XQ KQTARTQK XF PGWQHT, IBJQTT WQ
WLT ORHTG XQQB KQTARTQK XF WRNTQJO.

. . . .
283.

CFEN DQOIFMC PWNF DQES ESO WDQFN HXDSFII WC
DQO IXSI, CWN DQWR END DQF WSMO WSF DQWR YESID
SFLFN FIYEKF.

. . . .
284.

VJ VF DNX TVBIF JPRJ TRYO NF XVMP.

. . . .

285.

KS KL QFSSFC SB DFS SYF LSOCS BH O CFEMFLS
SYOX SB HBGGBA KS.

....

286.

SR RSJ FRMJH CAH QRKSODZ LJQNKHJ HCJ AH XDJNO,
LKO LJQNKHJ HCJ AH CAH RYS.

....

287.

WEX YXDW MBPPV WEZW WEF DPIJ UD SZJA UD WEF
ZYUJUWF WP SPHWUHIX UH WEUHX PTH SPAMZHF.

....

288.

XH XE SUQCHXICF HA NXUFW HA Q FQV, HA Q DCFUD,
AD HA Q VXEUD JQT.

....

289.

LCSIDWHGNJ DSXUX TGXUDJ KAGZ XAU YPXZ CUNSOUC
WF KGJX XZWDD YSCU TGXU.

. . . .
290.

RYUBG VL XIMY OIJ IC UB URCXWL I WULX.

. . . .
291.

JI GJU KQ QIXLYLBI NYUW LMP MIKEJDUY JLQ
NLCCIM LGLP NYUW BJI GJUCI RUWWOMKBP.

. . . .
292.

FUP HMEB AUYQU YH YDQVXVZBP MR VDLPG CVS
ZP DMF RPPZBP, ZEF XMHHPHHPN MR HFGMDLPG
YCXEBHPH.

. . . .

293.

UNYMY FB SPUNFSI IMTSR   UNTU FB SPU TABP WTAE.

. . . .

294.

RXHCSAXB DI OZSM PES PDOC ZS SD DXBCH VEK
XBES GK RXQMKZSA MZJZACSXJK ESM
DGRCHWZSA SEXQHC.

. . . .

295.

YK QDCK GLVKEB MKLLKE MW MKDETHN YTLV LVKQ, DHO
YGEBK MW ITHOTHN IDFUL.

. . . .

296.

YHDHC FMY EIHCH QH FSWCMJH AIHCH EIHCH ZV
YSE OHMFH.

. . . .

297.

MO VRJ BRJIF WLZA RGWAP NARNIA OAAI HPLGAOJI

GR VRJ, VRJ DJXG ERG REIV WAIN GWAD, TJG

IRZA GWAD.

. . . .
298.

BRUSU DQ GX YUDZ XYUS L QBLS.

. . . .
299.

V PVM OYBWUE OLVME WSZKFYL, VME MBL AG

JGSL WSZKFYL AC BLYGZO.

. . . .
300.

MKWK YP UQ YQRUJKW VMUV PMEXTJ FK OKV EQ VMK

LWEQVYKW.

. . . .

301.

MAX VA JA UDDO-BPXGTAO ICXF VN STCABOW, PBO
VCMO PBO APWN ICXF VN ABAVCAW.

. . . .

302.

OKXW PHI SWI HIOIPHXWIO UGH AWQXW AI PHI VGHE,
SWPS AI OWGKNB UQEB PNN SWI SQLI PNNGSSIB KO
OWGHS.

. . . .

303.

DBH UBFOZV S JWIG DBWN BWAAGKU, DBSZG LH UFOZ
SU WXFCG SN?

. . . .

304.

FWTHUJS EN FUHSQTB GW MHSNSHPS EGNSBQ, URC
HSUCL GW SRCTHS XOUG EN SPEB ER UMMSUHURFS
WRBL.

. . . .

305.

DXUEE HAO AMZ THAPELGQL OXUO QAG YD AMZ WUTLZ,
RUOXLZ, UHG QMUZGYUH, RZLL MD RZAW QZYLR AZ
RLUZ?

. . . .

306.

IW IYG NIW ALRJWGN LE APOWG BIL GHEEWMG RLN
NPTW NL DW ALGN.

. . . .

307.

P IPVV VSOOSZ ZJ JZSO VPLSNUK.

. . . .

308.

EIIQHAOO FIHOKOYO JBKHUX KH RKOPKHE YI TAFIJA
EIIQ.

. . . .

309.

DWTB VGBXJTWB YXI IBMBW YBXJB, IAW KB DTWIBZ
OIDA VXOI.

. . . .

310.

PR BTQPEEPTA ZH IPUK PT ZLK DHITPTA, UYO ZH
ZLOUKER, P YQYNK ZH SH ZLK QHIN HR Y DYT.

. . . .

311.

XW WXJ BD WHXJP WL KXWUOJPD HBAA.

. . . .

312.

GDY KQ ACMGAIY SKCAQRWDCY XAYRVKY
JCEDO, JCF HDIJKQD AY AQ KQDMKG, CVY HDIJKQD
ODNDCED AQ QXDDY.

. . . .

313.

AQ TAM AOKKBQI ZM KQWVC VF MNPBYVZBMF IAMTI VF

OFTBPPBFYFQII ZM KQXVBF OFHQK BZ - TABRA BI

BFYKVZBZOHQ.

. . . .
314.

YWW SCF YOC LWYTFWG IQEFJ XQHCXDCO.

. . . .
315.

JZ IFPYZA WBWPMDZYM OL FL KPSWC FL JZ IFPYZA

AZDZYM.

. . . .
316.

KNI PZLI RBA PZCC XI DCBF KM RBQQO BAF NBEI

YNZCFQIA, GMQ NI NBF QBKNIQ AMK CZEI BK BCC

KNBA CZEI BCMAI.

. . . .

317.

VO ZSS PZLO SONGWAO MRA VPZQ VO VNGP QR ER.

. . . .

318.

VBPTV LE UNPBTQDW, HEJ MQDLQOQ VYHV UNP HBQ

IHDCLEF LE VYQ BLFYV IHU.

. . . .

319.

FBAVP POTZ XKVO BANPOKAW XTCVU POBA SUBPO PT

PON UAUQN? LU BP UBVU. OU XKEE SKU URUA KJ NTZ

YUUI GZKUP.

. . . .

320.

RTV QXJ QRVM GRNV BRN YUV VQEAXYVQ GXT YUXT

YUV IRTSVMY IPBV BRN YUVG ETYXESUY.

. . . .

321.

KGMJOGXQSJQQ FJWBZOQ SG EWPOZOXNJ.

. . . .

322.

TFKD IHY THYRM CV KLFKQVM HX XVVRAPN

YPMVW HCRANKDAHP XHW MH PHD KEEVBD.

. . . .

323.

BDNSN TU HQ ITUZSLJN TH DLRTHZ QKS QATHTQHU

JDLHZN MTBD BDN JTSJKOUBLHJNU.

. . . .

324.

DCB CQEOR GVZ VBC IBVRUCZ; RUCZCGVZC

RCIMU RUCD VZ WCIZ SERU RUCD.

. . . .

325.

OTEX BYE YANXE JXL TLF HXEDX ANX OYJJYL GEYANXENYYF.

. . . .

326.

UNFUS VAICFYNH EB OUHYDL, ATOIOAI EB PTTYPDOIQ UA YRUYNIPDH.

. . . .

327.

YNQ BEM EPGC YL XL GQO HLLX, SKY YNPC PY IEOOLY EIILGTBPCN KOBQCC YNQD EJQ MPBBPOH.

. . . .

328.

GTY UJT GURT LFJ ATBHEYM TUNA FCATJ.

. . . .

329.

HJ TVGA CH DJ SCGA EJ HAFPADH ISVFS QJZ
IJZTK EJD SCGA BEJIE DJ QJZP AEAOVAH.

. . . .
330.

XUMHCMCFV XURSJ, NUWOIACFV HIYULSP, RFX
LUMSLRCFCFV WDMS, SJUMU SJLUU VCYU VLURS
XUWCVJS.

. . . .
331.

PRUG BF CBLHO BAXKWZHOGJV BF JTFG
EWJXUDJV, UOZ ATKH FT ITK ZTBOC OT CTTZ GRUO
ITK AUQBOC OT KHGWKO.

. . . .
332.

N FNL RNLLBV PKVNWL ZWT YWTCBF, GLJKTT ZK ZNT
SPWKLCT JWUK ZWFTKJS.

. . . .

333.

UYIF JCMVRSVMUUO RWF KFH NSRW NWYK RWO UYR SA

VMAR.

. . . .

334.

TVNE PDHUGNBCH AVDQRHRAVZ YRGC EVNW

HCCXDWU NAAQNOHC?

. . . .

335.

GRRV CDLYDI: LYUPU DJ LYU WRZILQDI RW XRRN

CYDEY CDGG QGCQKJ XZJY WRPLY, DW LYRZ CDGL

QGCQKJ NDX.

. . . .

336.

PR EPF EFXIZ HR DCZRQRCZRCB KXGB GRRT

SFL CFBPDCU JCZ SIRR SLFK CFBPDCU EPDYP

ZRQRCZG FC FBPRLG.

. . . .

337.

BSW NEVW UKA NEDD LKFIGA UMRS, KAI VKXW UKAZ
VGMDV OWRKMVW BSWZ KFW RKLKODW GQ OWEAY
SWKDWI.

. . . .

338.

WGRUSWB DGZYI FHGW PWA ZPW VUSDU UY SI WGR
EGQZYK RG CYPQ.

. . . .

339.

WTBS XLJXRRXHJX AM WTBS SXPMTH; PQTSH GUPG PHQ
FPZX AG KXPBGADBR.

. . . .

340.

VF HQJF DTS KGB L WILHH XLSB TD BMF BQIF, LRA
BMF SFILQRQRZ XLSB QW RTB BT KF NLHHFA HQDF.

. . . .

341.

SZAG EJWCH OYZTR EXFHJS, HXH KRYG AJK FWLLJFY
KRYG RZH ZCOYZHG ZOOXNYH KRYOY.

. . . .

342.

WS TD MRRZ NWR WJD ISSQ RY RCWSZD, JIQ WJD IRC
TI WTODSEY JEE WS NJICD.

. . . .

343.

HRCFZB BHXBRZI GRH CK GRH.

. . . .

344.

TPL PT LXUXH QV DX VUXHAVWX DZ TPL.

. . . .

345.

BP UZMR YHIVEPSO HO JPLBFIR BP VHMR BURS,
MHLBFR.

. . . .
346.

UBZNA SYKV PFACYCMC FK RYAXAVCC NAX UNEZFAW,
NAX YC UVSX MFOVMUVE KFE ZBMBNS UVSG, AFM DW
MVEEFE, DBM DW SFJV.

. . . .
347.

FNB DHGF MPUUPT BNTUF NHT BFREP UN IKNB BFXU
BP QFNHEY YN, UFXK BFXU FXQ MPPK XETPXYS YNKP!

. . . .
348.

FM XK AXQW GFV BMZTK QVCFXQW ZQE YVQWK BVT
QVCFXQW. MPMTSVQM DZS WXPM FXDKMYB CFM
AXQWEVD VB QVRYM CFVJWFCK.

. . . .

349.

VKY ODIYOV JXDR VX ZMJVHY MO JYGYLVDLWY.

. . . .
350.

USD ACNUS OSNMS DQGDMUY ZDOCZXY NY UK WD

MKBELDZDX WR USDT.

. . . .
351.

SCAB UNFYWFQ.

. . . .
352.

PH ZHANSZC ELA YNVA SQ LQKTLI AH XKZ.

. . . .

353.

GAI DSPPYXLP SWI SP FSH PIWRSLGP SP KISHIWP.

. . . .

354.

GJTR-REFHV TQX MCV OTNVG HT HEV ZMHFVJH.

. . . .

355.

UBAABY OBDKB NYSXB VCHVCSGEBJ AEDC

NWCJBXC AEB SCCWNBCA.

. . . .

356.

DC BDP FJPBA HDMH ICJ MXC JPH VPXJ BRAC, VQH

DMYC HP VCGPIC AP, BRTT JCYCX VC MJSXK BRHD HDC

CXXRJS.

. . . .

357.

ZDA VTA HLADAIV VTPZSTVJZOOK XIE

FZDVOK, JPL OCJA CD DTPLV.

. . . .

358.

SIUS YIQTI QV BCS PCCH OCJ SIK VYUJL QV BCS

PCCH OCJ SIK RKK.

. . . .

359.

SX DSV ZVEWAW SJW ZJCAS NCJRXW SJPWXMQ VH DSEA

ZXMVHYW AV VASXCW.

. . . .

360.

PKOPT TZPUX SUEZD.

. . . .

361.

YPBY FUWEDNW ZYWWYOB UB P ZUGUVQ XYPWE PVX

TNOUPZ.

. . . .

362.

UW XTW JTWXMWG ZHT MLW NXOW HZ SXBOEBG, MH QW

VNWZVR MH WXJL HMLWT.

. . . .

363.

ET LDCYH UCDDCPT SQCTZ PQC UDZZ UYCB QZY, TC

FT LYESFSVKZ LFRZJ BCTS YFWQDH SC SQCTZ PQC

SCDZYESZ FJLYESFSVKZ.

. . . .

364.

VQLUN ZF PBU XQQRF VTFPUO, ADP PBU KZFU

VTLF FRTEU.

. . . .

365.

DBKYTDZ TV AEVSO KYED KB UTVY NBO WSEKY.

. . . .
366.

MFUZ UZ PIQYRMUVE, MV APRNE MV DUZF MFRM

MFUEBZ ZFVQAI FRWWPE RZ MFPS IV.

. . . .
367.

GJGOU ERBF VE DOGYHGI HR YDDGNH MWYH VE HOBG,

OGKGDH MWYH VE XYFEG, YSI IRBAH MWYH VE

BSDGOHYVS.

. . . .
368.

MVB FOICEZ FMLBSD VQENL TEBQMSZ MVB UEAOTYABE.

. . . .

369.

KPQ UKS PR EVSWSAZM JF DSI, JFFJXA UPFK APYMYZRRZR, JYM KPR UVJFK UPTT XZJRZ.

. . . .

370.

CP KJP EKLP RSJ ISSQPJKNVSB, OVAP NWP WKBLG KBL RPPN.

. . . .

371.

EPSWYEL MPUC APBU SP CSBUELSWUE SWU QWNBNQSUB YE IYBSJU, NEM RBUU YS RBPA IYQU, SWNE SWU CPQYUSO PR SWU LPPM.

. . . .

372.

JNIW PWTNBWDA YMMTA YDMI ZDNWY, KCP DWKAMC SNAW IWC.

. . . .

373.

UV QUF PVMBVLVE AUSA QV SIV SMM PFIR FT WFK

JSR RVLVI AUBRG FT UBOEVMT OVSRMC FI

PSEVMC.

. . . .

374.

AP CPH HOKCV QKVF OKS MOP MUPCLG HOFF, PU EG

OF MPXQA OEDF HOFF, JXH GFF MOEH KG UFRXKUFA JB

HOF HUXHO.

. . . .

375.

HCUULIE SA KIN PTSKUL DW ATNSAHWSKP, DRN DW

CUANCTSKSKP, IRC LUASCUA.

. . . .

376.

PC HPK IMXT KWU CMNP FMX MT BS BU HCVC M IBSC

HBII ACBUPCV SCMV AKV IKAQ SKV UPC YKVVKH.

. . . .

385.

PAN JABLNKXN BX PJK EPHHPA ZIKNAO.

. . . .

386.

HFXLOF NP PFFURDW BNXLOV BTF YOIFU LE BTFC VN

BNXLOV NBTFOE.

. . . .

387.

DCGNNMSMST YMTNSUQ NAM TUVCT UD FMP JQ

JCEPYEPH NAMES MQMT.

. . . .

388.

SMOKPA OPPRH ZJUUZP, YMU CAJRP OPPRH VMGS.

. . . .

377.

ASQNZPZASG KLQYSLH BTTLAYP KZH HLMLTYP

BKG ZKL, ERY PSQKLP JZH BNN.

. . . .

378.

NZPS FDN VSUUHDYIA BSVNGC; UPD NZPS

XYVZHVN NP THQPOH APPK NPOPDDPX, DFNZHD NZFI

NP TH VP NPKFC.

. . . .

379.

EY WTFST YWR RW OS UYBTP MERC UYPOWFP, PWL

ACWLJF QUTFWY SNSTPOWFP. PWLT

KWTBENSYSAA EA FLS RW PWLT TUGS.

. . . .

380.

T NHTLBPAPV UHAPV VBHL BP OAL STD SHJJ, SOHP

OH IANHKML OAL AFZWJLHL BPJD MB TKMABPL BY

ZWUJAK UHPHYAM.

. . . .

381.

CR RSSM CR C KZNTB NR ESWM OS JR, NO NR MS
TSMHGW NM SJW DSPGW MSO OS TSIG NO CMB KCWG QSW
NO.

. . . .
382.

JZYLO DLAUZH LZY UDOYX HSUGIO KT KYGXJ JGAYX
HIUNIT LXC HLCIT, LXC LH GD OBYT NYZY
ZYDEHYC.

. . . .
383.

NMKP VERSLYHOEI WECH, SKHHCH KNKG, NMKP
SCBHLKHOEI WECH, CIWLBCH.

. . . .
384.

GI GU MGQS B VSUSAISA IJ ZMSS BEBC ZAJO UJDGBM
MBEU.

. . . .

389.

XJDSVJY GJET-YJGZJUS XWY ZYAKJXUJ DG GVWRX CN
VDP RVW YJIKDEN SVDXHG VDPGJET KJGZDGJK.

. . . .

390.

LYZ GEPVL FKD XG GPEZTMVYEQ EV
ZCAKFELU.

. . . .

391.

ZCT ZQ DNZYKC NCQPXB TQPC YQPMK, XQZ YKCBM
QU QOKX, RPZ ZCQQGM QU UCSKXBM.

. . . .

392.

CNP RFPYCPAC EYACP DU CHWP HA CNP XPQYK
ENHGN CYTPA YEYK DJF MFPAPLC, ENHQP
MFDWHAHLR Y UJCJFP.

. . . .

393.

HDUOQS GJC ZS ZYUL DL JLC VXJKS.

. . . .

394.

MGCDTDL UGRYU, CL JDUPLDU, MGVA PU YCA

PY GPU CMY QCMDL, FVYYCA OD DPAGDL

XVPAGXRI CL XLDD.

. . . .

395.

UNJXIO, WMURWPMXR MS GOI MZU ZPRQML NUQ YONXJH,

GNR WIONJOQ XR NR MYROIKOIR MS EMSJH

RCOWJNWEOR.

. . . .

396.

HE HC GWCOIS EQ RQCZ QOI QLV HVVQXZVXZ IGEAZI

EAGV EQ SQ AGID EQ QEAZI MZQMRZ.

. . . .

397.

NA TZEM YXAOS XMO YN ZW SAG NYU CAF. NA NKMYP
DA SAG YN ZW XMO JMYBG CAF.

. . . .
398.

IAPL HAF KF ZFI DPPW UICOGOZB IF EKGEZYP
XEQQ NEYD; ZF FZP XOZKU AOU WCFBCPUU EU AP QPXI
OI.

. . . .
399.

MTR MJEUI WGX NTVUL XUEUL HT CUH PJWIUCZ
SU IUNGLGHUR ZLTW HPU MLUGH VPTCU.

. . . .
400.

YOHRYDOQCS KQNDR XOQDLZR; BZNDORQCS
YOHNDR CPDA.

. . . .

1: E=S	25: R=N
2: U=S	26: M=H
3: O=R	27: R=T
4: L=E	28: Y=E
5: Y=I	29: W=I
6: C=O	30: D=E
7: L=E	31: H=I
8: P=O	32: V=S
9: M=R	33: B=E
10: M=H	34: Y=D
11: I=E	35: M=E
12: I=S	36: G=E
13: B=E	37: L=E
14: T=O	38: K=I
15: E=T	39: K=I
16: M=T	40: S=N
17: R=E	41: G=T
18: A=O	42: O=A
19: X=T	43: C=N
20: X=A	44: I=E
21: I=O	45: G=A
22: V=I	46: V=E
23: R=E	47: A=E
24: I=A	48: X=I

49: D=S	73: T=E
50: Y=A	74: T=E
51: C=S	75: N=A
52: C=H	76: R=S
53: Q=S	77: S=A
54: T=S	78: A=I
55: N=A	79: N=O
56: V=O	80: M=O
57: Y=A	81: A=S
58: D=H	82: U=E
59: A=O	83: Y=S
60: L=E	84: D=E
61: Y=T	85: Y=T
62: I=E	86: A=E
63: H=O	87: R=O
64: G=T	88: I=A
65: Z=S	89: R=T
66: Q=N	90: X=E
67: S=H	91: J=E
68: X=N	92: T=E
69: G=E	93: R=H
70: I=E	94: Z=S
71: A=N	95: C=T
72: W=R	96: R=T

97: S=T	121: P=T
98: E=O	122: H=O
99: K=O	123: H=O
100: T=E	124: Y=R
101: K=T	125: B=T
102: F=A	126: Y=A
103: O=A	127: Q=E
104: V=E	128: A=I
105: R=T	129: T=O
106: L=H	130: U=E
107: M=S	131: L=T
108: H=A	132: N=E
109: W=S	133: R=S
110: S=T	134: C=A
111: M=S	135: D=E
112: V=E	136: A=H
113: H=A	137: A=H
114: F=T	138: Q=E
115: A=E	139: X=R
116: Y=I	140: T=E
117: I=O	141: U=N
118: F=T	142: E=T
119: A=T	143: L=A
120: P=E	144: P=H

145: I=O	169: P=E
146: E=I	170: E=H
147: Z=E	171: W=N
148: S=O	172: T=E
149: W=N	173: Z=O
150: L=N	174: Y=E
151: Y=A	175: U=T
152: B=A	176: H=S
153: C=E	177: F=N
154: P=O	178: J=N
155: H=E	179: Q=A
156: L=E	180: A=H
157: F=R	181: K=E
158: L=S	182: F=E
159: K=E	183: S=T
160: R=N	184: H=E
161: J=T	185: J=E
162: O=E	186: C=N
163: J=S	187: R=I
164: O=E	188: L=O
165: O=E	189: S=H
166: I=A	190: N=T
167: M=E	191: X=T
168: F=A	192: C=S

193: M=E	217: G=T
194: G=I	218: M=E
195: Y=T	219: T=I
196: D=S	220: J=N
197: L=R	221: V=S
198: F=I	222: Q=T
199: N=T	223: O=I
200: U=A	224: K=S
201: U=O	225: R=O
202: Z=N	226: Q=A
203: W=I	227: R=E
204: K=E	228: E=O
205: E=T	229: U=A
206: Y=H	230: N=O
207: B=H	231: J=A
208: C=E	232: E=I
209: O=T	233: F=H
210: H=N	234: W=H
211: S=O	235: I=A
212: M=A	236: C=A
213: O=T	237: L=I
214: Y=I	238: H=E
215: R=I	239: U=H
216: V=E	240: R=I

241: Y=A	265: T=N
242: O=E	266: H=A
243: Y=O	267: S=I
244: S=A	268: S=N
245: K=T	269: M=N
246: C=S	270: U=N
247: L=S	271: R=I
248: E=N	272: H=N
249: O=S	273: W=H
250: X=N	274: F=A
251: F=N	275: G=O
252: K=O	276: M=T
253: D=T	277: S=E
254: Y=O	278: J=H
255: J=I	279: T=O
256: O=T	280: K=E
257: X=S	281: Z=H
258: I=N	282: T=S
259: G=O	283: D=T
260: F=T	284: F=S
261: E=N	285: F=E
262: W=T	286: H=S
263: D=T	287: U=I
264: J=H	288: H=T

289: U=E
290: U=I
291: I=E
292: H=S
293: T=A
294: X=T
295: L=T
296: C=R
297: R=O
298: S=R
299: V=A
300: V=T
301: O=D
302: W=H
303: W=A
304: U=A
305: U=A
306: L=O
307: P=I
308: O=S
309: I=N
310: H=O
311: X=N
312: Q=S

313: F=N
314: Y=A
315: F=A
316: I=E
317: V=W
318: V=T
319: P=T
320: Y=T
321: Q=S
322: V=E
323: H=N
324: R=T
325: Y=O
326: I=N
327: P=I
328: U=A
329: A=E
330: S=T
331: O=N
332: K=E
333: W=H
334: C=E
335: Y=H
336: C=N

337: K=A	361: Y=E
338: G=O	362: X=A
339: P=A	363: Z=E
340: B=T	364: F=S
341: H=D	365: K=T
342: S=E	366: F=H
343: H=N	367: H=T
344: P=I	368: E=R
345: B=T	369: P=I
346: A=N	370: K=A
347: P=E	371: S=T
348: V=O	372: N=I
349: V=T	373: S=A
350: S=H	374: O=H
351: N=A	375: U=E
352: Z=N	376: K=O
353: S=A	377: K=N
354: H=T	378: N=T
355: C=N	379: T=R
356: J=N	380: A=I
357: A=E	381: N=I
358: S=T	382: L=A
359: W=S	383: K=A
360: Z=A	384: B=A

385: A=N	409:
386: N=O	410:
387: T=S	411:
388: R=D	412:
389: G=S	413:
390: Z=E	414:
391: C=R	415:
392: C=T	416:
393: S=E	417:
394: C=O	418:
395: O=E	419:
396: Z=E	420:
397: Y=A	421:
398: F=O	422:
399: T=O	423:
400: O=R	424:
401:	425:
402:	426:
403:	427:
404:	428:
405:	429:
406:	430:
407:	431:
408:	432:

1.

Wouldst thou subject all things to thyself,

subject thyself to wisdom.

2.

Act well to present friends speak well of

absent ones.

3.

Which had you rather give up--yourself, or

some of your troubles?

4.

Who is nobly born? He who is by nature

virtuous. It is the character that makes

the noble.

5.

I shall give nothing for which I would be
ashamed to ask.

6.

Choose not the most pleasant, but the most
useful of physicians and of friends.

7.

It may happen that he who returns a favor is
ungrateful, and he is grateful who does not.

8.

From Diognetus I learned to endure freedom of
speech. ,

9.

If the wrong-doer be weak, spare him; if he

be strong, spare yourself.

10.

The philosopher will not be the enemy, but the

teacher, of sinners.

11.

Let no one suppose that I would check charity

let it go where it will, but not wander to

and fro.

12.

Philosophy will give us the greatest of

blessings--freedom from regret.

13.

Do you wish to be useful, or to be

praised?

14.

He who cultivates wisdom cultivates the

knowledge of God.

15.

Whatever I can do ought to be directed to this

end alone--usefulness to the community.

16.

We need amusements, but there should be some

work in them, that even from them we may get

good.

17.

Let thy efforts and exertions be turned
toward acting for the public good.

18.

Pure, not only from forbidden pleasures,
but from useless ones.

19.

If thou be able, teach others what is right
if thou be not, remember that meekness
was given thee for this.

20.

My country is wherever I am happy; and that
depends on the man, not the place.

21.

He will blame fortune alone for others sins.

22.

Of what use is your reading, if it does

not give you peace?

23.

Prodigality is never noble, and especially

not in charity.

24.

Why not take care of your short life, and

make it pleasant for others, and also for

yourself?

25.

My word is as my country to me, and even

dearer, if anything can be.

26.

He is wise who rejoices in what he has, and

does not grieve for what he has not.

27.

However my brother treats me, I must do

my duty by him that is all that need concern

me.

28.

Remembering our benefactors needs no

time, or skill, or opportunity, but only

good intentions.

29.

It is our inconstancy, in beginning one thing
after another, that makes life short.

30.

He is an ingrate who repays a kindness
without giving interest.

31.

Virtue unbinds the chain of the soul, by
teaching, experience and exercise.

32.

Love wisdom, and this love will arm you
against the strongest foes.

33.

Justice considers only the good of others,

and desires nothing but to be of use.

34.

Good fortune is good intentions, good

impulses, and good deeds.

35.

She who can be compelled knows not how to die.

36.

Love sometimes harms, but friendship always

helps.

37.

Think of pleasures in excess as punishments.

38.

Give the kindness for its own sake thinking

only of the receivers interests.

39.

I must keep reading, in order to keep

dissatisfied with myself.

40.

Wisdom looks on every man as a friend, but

folly will not even look on a friend as a

man.

41.

The ingrate is pleased for the time, the grateful man for ever.

42.

Do not fear that you have wasted your study if you have taught yourself.

43.

There is only one days difference between the insane and the angry.

44.

It is better to advise than to reproach.

45.

Nobody but a madman would be angry with brute beasts, which do not know that they are injuring us.

46.

No one who is a lover of money, pleasure, or fame, is also a lover of mankind, but only he who is a lover of virtue.

47.

The highest and holiest ideas are best discussed in common, and by combining various mens ideas.

48.

It is a little thing not to refuse work; demand it.

49.

Glory should not be pursued by us, but follow us.

50.

What is wisdom? Always to wish for the same things.

51.

Reason never needs the help of violent and reckless impulses over which she has no authority.

52.

Virtue is the same, whether she is reached through joys or griefs.

53.

Sickness is a hindrance to the body, but not
to the will, unless that yields.

54.

He who seeks true glory wishes not so much to
be praised by voices as by hearts.

55.

We should be neither squeamish nor abject
in taking favors.

56.

Most people seek in the tavern for that
pleasure which is to be found in labor.

57.

Always remember that very little is needed

for living a happy life.

58.

The wise man considers to whom he gives,

rather than what he gives.

59.

The wise man has a country worthy of him,

the universe, out of which he cannot go.

60.

Let private interests yield to public, the

mortal to the eternal.

61.

He is not honest who cares for anything in
this virtue except itself.

62.

To be angry, even for those dear to us, is
the sign, not of a noble soul, but of a
weak one.

63.

Mans nature is to do good and assist others
and comply with their wishes.

64.

Satisfy conscience and do not work for
reputation, but let this make itself,
though it be worse than we deserve.

65.

Follow this sound and safe rule of life--to indulge the body just so much as its health requires.

66.

Put all thy joy and satisfaction in passing from one philanthropic action to another, think of God.

67.

If he be your friend, he has done what was not intended; if he be your enemy, what might have been foreseen.

68.

Animals who lack reason should be treated nobly and magnanimously.

69.

My mother taught me to keep myself not only

from doing wrong, but even from imagining it.

70.

To love our neighbor is a property which shows

a soul endowed with reason.

71.

The wise mans joy is woven so well as not

to be broken by any accident.

72.

Never make it either necessary or

profitable for your child to ask for

anything abjectly.

73.

He who cultivates others virtue cultivates also his own.

74.

he wise man needs much, but wants nothing; the fool needs nothing, but wants everything.

75.

As weapons to chained hands, so are precepts to sinful souls.

76.

the friendless.

77.

Do nothing without a purpose, and let that always be some public end.

78.

In the perfection of our reason lies all the happiness of life.

79.

The pride of not being proud is the most hard to bear.

80.

He who is good and wise never quarrels with anybody, but tries to keep others out of strife.

81.

Labor nourishes noble souls.

82.

Often our duty is to be just and reputed
infamous.

83.

He is free who arises above all injuries,
and finds all his joys within himself.

84.

Thrasea used to say, He who hates vice hates
mankind.

85.

Where there is contentment there is
no poverty. It is not he who has little, but
he who desires more, that is poor.

86.

Among useful things is money, not in
superfluity, but in quantity sufficient for
all moderate desires.

87.

Receive what is in your own power with
courage; and what is not, with caution.

88.

Never be careless, even about what is called
unimportant.

89.

If you would judge justly, esteem neither

parties nor pleaders, but the case itself.

90.

He who repents of his sins is already almost

innocent.

91.

Chastity, whose loss is every virtues ruin.

92.

Prosperity invites our fidelity adversity

demands it.

93.

Live with thy inferiors as thou wouldst have thy superiors live with thee.

94.

It is not poverty, but covetousness, that causes sorrow. It is not wealth, but philosophy, that gives security.

95.

I shall take the world as my country.

96.

Liberty is not to be had gratis; if she be worth much to us, all things else will have little value.

97.

It is madness to think that we fix an end to passions which we cannot control at their beginnings.

98.

I do my duty; other things trouble me not.

99.

Do not so much fear being disgraced by public opinion as by the truth.

100.

Nothing is so honorable as a great soul; but that soul is not great which can be shaken by either fear or grief.

101.

The true philosopher, unless prevented, will

serve the state.

102.

The safety of life demands that I do what

is just with my whole soul, and say what is

true.

103.

When you have advanced far enough to

reverence yourself, you may dismiss all

mentors.

104.

Man becomes better and nobler by making a

right use of all that comes to pass.

105.

The height of purity or impurity is in the

soul.

106.

Flee from the friendship of the wicked and the

hatred of the good. (

107.

Never does the suspicious man lack

evidence.

108.

Let us honor humanity, and cause no danger or

fear to anyone.

109.

A mans worth is that of those things about

which he is busy.

110.

Nothing so favors temperance in all

things as the thought how short and uncertain

life is.

111.

This is grand, to act always like the same

man.

112.

What madness to be dragged along by the

divine will, rather than follow it!

113.

The chief end of a rational creature is
the social life.

114.

What we bear is not so important as how we
bear it.

115.

It is base to say, and baser still to write,
what we do not feel.

116.

If your kindness be returned, there is
gain if it be not, there is no loss.

117.

Study not to know more, but better.

118.

What will be the reward of our studies? The

noblest that could be wished: the knowledge

of nature.

119.

Do not make thyself either the tyrant or

the slave of any man.

120.

True courage will avoid danger, but not fear

it.

121.

Better be despised for candor, than tortured

perpetually by attempts to deceive.

122.

Instead of asking Fortune for her gifts,

ask thyself not to ask for them.

123.

Severus commanded me to love those who dwell

with me.

124.

Will you not bear with your brother, who has

God for his ancestor and is of your own

heavenly race?

125.

It is best to keep the feasts of the people

without their excesses.

126.

A stomach which can wait patiently, and endure

rough treatment, is an important condition of

liberty.

127.

When thou wouldst be joyful, call to mind

the good qualities of those who live with

thee.

128.

Delight in acts of kindness is our

nearest approach to the divine.

129.

He who will not forbid sin commands it.

130.

If you see anybody wail and complain, call him
a slave, though he be clad in purple.

131.

Do not make an idol of your clothes, and you
will not be angry at the thief.

132.

Thou art a man set at thy post for the
benefit of the state.

133.

Whether the slave has become so by conquest

or by purchase, the masters title is bad.

134.

Obey that law of nature which makes your

interest the universal, and the universal one

you own.

135.

He who can tell his dreams has awaked; and

he who call tell his faults has repented.

136.

The duty of the philosopher is to

protect, not his wine, his oil, or his body,

but his reason.

137.

There is no happiness where there is any
fear.

138.

I will show you how to make a love-potion
without either drugs or spells: If you would be
loved, love.

139.

The best cure for anger is delay.

140.

Let nothing be more precious to thee than
the truth.

141.

Does any one hate me? I will be kind and friendly to every one.

142.

Everything has two handles, and can be carried by one of them, but not by the other.

143.

Nothing is more natural to man than kindness.

144.

He is wicked who does not practice that chastity which he requires from his wife.

145.

We must conquer our passions, not by strategy, but by main force; not by slight wounds, but by a deadly charge.

146.

The wise man looks upon himself as the citizen and soldier of the universe.

147.

How much better to heal an injury than to avenge it!

148.

Simple and modest is the work of philosophy; may I not be tempted into pride!

149.

We come into fortunes power, when we think anything but virtue good.

150.

Never be contented with a superficial apprehension of anything.

151.

A brave and wise man should not flee from life.

152.

Make your daily food, not of expense and trouble, but of frugality and joy.

153.

If you would live for yourself, live for others.

154.

We may think ourselves free from lust when we ask God for nothing which we cannot pray for openly.

155.

Who has most? He who desires least.

156.

He who takes gratefully has paid the first instalment of his debt.

157.

In the upper air there is neither cloud nor storm, and so in the lofty soul there is always peace.

158.

Mind, knowledge, right reason--here seek the essence of goodness.

159.

The Cynic loves those who beat him, and is a father and brother toward all men.

160.

The wise man will not punish offenders for his own revenge, but for their amendment.

161.

Feeling is king when it seeks the right, but

when it is unruly it takes a hateful name,

and becomes tyrant.

162.

Should a gift not prove a benefit, it would

yet be ungrateful not to return it, as if it

were.

163.

Wise men resist pleasures; fools are

enslaved.

164.

Thrasea used to say that we should take the

side not only of our friends, but of

165.

Have thy slaves honor, rather than fear, thee. Punish them only with words.

166.

I was taught to endure labor, to want little, and to do things myself.

167.

Let nothing be more precious to thee than truth.

168.

Wisdom shows her strength by her peace amid trouble, like an army encamped in safety in a hostile land.

169.

Not yet dost thou see that prudence is all

contained in justice.

170.

I had rather show you my feelings than speak

them.

171.

Be like a headland, standing firm against

the waves that beat against it continually,

and calming the raging sea.

172.

Walk in the country, so that thy mind may

expand and exalt itself in the fresh air and

free sky.

173.

Fortune has not such long arms as we think;
she seizes on no one who is not clinging to
her.

174.

Consider not how many, but what sort of
people you please.

175.

The weak grow strong in union, but the mighty
perish by discord.

176.

As the touchstone tries gold, but is not
itself tried by it, so is he who has the power
of judging justly.

177.

We must learn virtue by unlearning vice.

178.

Fight against the beginnings of evil;

but anger begins with thinking that we are

injured.

179.

How easy to drive away every thought that is

troublesome, or unfriendly, and be at

peace at once.

180.

Before thy marriage, keep thyself pure with

all thy might.

181.

Advise a friend in private; praise him openly.

182.

What is more pleasant than to be so dear to your wife as to be on this account dearer to yourself?

183.

It is vain to hope that virtue will descend into our souls by chance.

184.

That which satisfies us is never too little, and that which does not is never much.

185.

Fortify thyself in contentment, for this

is a fortress which cannot be taken easily.

186.

Does any one sin against thee? He has sinned

against himself.

187.

Peace with all mankind, but war with vice.

188.

Nature commands me to do good to all men,

whether they be bound or free.

189.

He who spares the bad wrongs the good.

190.

Often it is easier to renounce utterly than

to enjoy moderately.

191.

Often the friends give exactly what the

enemies wish.

192.

Fortune conquers us, unless she is

conquered utterly.

193.

No one who knows his obligations, and
heartily wishes to discharge them, need
think himself outdone in kindness.

194.

Nothing that happens injures me, unless I
take it as an evil; and it is in my power not
to take it so.

195.

It is easy to keep base desires from entering,
but hard to drive them out.

196.

He who repays a kindness because he hopes for
another is ungrateful.

197.

Fear and penitence for those who can neither

rule nor obey their desires.

198.

From early youth we can give ourselves to

looking at the truth, finding a rule of life,

and obeying it quietly.

199.

It is best that those who are helped should

not know their benefactor, for the

secrecy increases the gift.

200.

Read much, but not many books.

201.

We should not expose our feeble souls to wine,

beauty, or flattery.

202.

The noblest virtue is not fostered by

incense and garlands, but by sweat and blood.

203.

I should be unjust, as well as ungrateful, if

I were not glad to have him who benefits me

benefit himself, also.

204.

Only that by which the character is made

better is good.

205.

Do not labor unwillingly, or

without regard to the common good.

206.

He who associates calmly with the wicked is one

of them himself.

207.

He who dies for love of wealth and pleasure

shows that he never had a right to live.

208.

The good man bears calmly much that is

not evil, except to those that take it ill.

209.

The soul has power to live most happily, if she will not be anxious about what is unimportant.

210.

No one is so high in fortune as not to need a friend all the more, because he needs nothing else.

211.

It is vicious either to trust nobody or to trust everybody.

212.

Philosophy teaches love of man, preaches peace, and calls on the whole human race to live in harmony.

213.

Throw away all anxiety about life, and so make it pleasant.

214.

It is our scorn for what can be had easily that makes all our life difficult.

215.

Better die than live ill.

216.

It is wonderful how much the mind is excited by moving the body.

217.

To act a part, or say or do anything insincere
or untrue, pollutes the soul.

218.

Man is created to live in society and for the
common good.

219.

Rejoice in what you have, and like
whatever times brings.

220.

Peculiarly manly is benevolence to our
fellow-men.

221.

The grandest of empires is to rule ones self.

222.

Let thy slaves laugh, or talk, or be silent, in

thy presence, as in that of the father of

the family.

223.

It is base to be outdone in kindness.

224.

He who studies the universe serves God.

225.

No other vice is so hostile to the harmony

of the human race as ingratitude.

226.

That man is never safe who can be moved by

injury or abuse.

227.

Nothing costs more than what is begged.

228.

The good and noble man does nothing for the

sake of appearances, but everything for the

sake of acting well.

229.

The same law of nature binds us all together.

230.

Give no judgment from any other tribunal,

before you have yourself been judged at

that of Justice.

231.

What a monster is he who rages at his

fellow-men!

232.

A kindness should be returned in the same

spirit in which it is bestowed.

233.

He is most ungrateful who forgets what has been given him.

234.

As thou thinkest most often, so will be thy character; for by the thoughts the soul is dyed.

235.

Calamity is opportunity for courage.

236.

There is a natural fellowship among men, and it ought in every way to be preserved.

237.

Every place is safe for him who dwells with justice.

238.

What is the first business of him who seeks wisdom? To cast away self-conceit.

239.

That harms not the citizen which does not harm the state.

240.

No one drives away vice, until in its place he accepts wisdom.

241.

No one is grateful for what he has extorted.

We find many ingrates, and we make more.

242.

Show me some one who is sick, in danger,

disgraced, dying, but yet happy. Show him,

for I long to see a Stoic!

243.

Virtue is the only thing which does not change,

so as to be sometimes good and sometimes bad.

244.

Treat men fraternally, because they are

endowed with reason.

245.

He will treat them as the doctor does his

patients; and what physician is angry with

a maniac?

246.

Not even the choicest friendship is free

from passions which may overshadow and disturb

thy sense of justice.

247.

Eloquence harms those whom it leads to love

itself and not its subjects.

248.

Gratitude returns intention for

intention, as well as act for act.

249.

A very little can satisfy our necessities, but nothing our desires.

250.

He who longs to wear gold and purple is poor, not by fortunes fault, but by his own.

251.

Fear nothing, but that thy mind should turn to something unworthy of a thinker and a citizen.

252.

No one is more ready to tread others under his feet than he who has become used to taking insults.

253.

He who gives ought to forget it immediately, but he who receives never.

254.

If you choose to keep your will in harmony with nature you are safe and free from care.

255.

Before we form a friendship we should criticize, but after forming it we should only trust.

256.

Only to the busy belongs the present.

257.

The arts serve life, but wisdom rules it.

258.

The mind that is free from passion is a

castle, and man has none more strong.

259.

He who follows after pleasure will not keep

himself from injustice.

260.

It is better to grow braver than more

learned, but neither can be done without the

other.

261.

To restrain lust in its beginning, think about
its end.

262.

Our object should be the good of the state and
of the community.

263.

To forget a kindness proves that we have
never kept it in our thoughts, or meant to
be grateful.

264.

He who gives when he is asked has waited too
long.

265.

The mind turns every obstacle into an aid.

266.

Experience has taught me not to ask advice when

I have made up my mind what to do.

267.

What would I have death find me doing?

Something benevolent, public-spirited, and

noble.

268.

We become happy by not needing happiness.

269.

Giving to a base man is neither noble nor

generous.

270.

If there were reason for beginning to be angry,

there would be none for ever ceasing to be.

271.

He yields to destiny, and consoles himself

by knowing that he is carried along with the

universe.

272.

He will be on his guard against his anger who

understands that it begins by injuring him

first of all.

273.

What must the soul of the angry man be, when
his face is so hideous?

274.

Nothing is so painful as long suspense. What
you add to the delay you take from the
gratitude.

275.

Nobody would give away his property to all
comers, as everybody gives away his life.

276.

Remember that to change thy mind, and follow
him who sets thee right, does not lessen
thy independence.

277.

Do not be ashamed of being helped, for thou

must do thy duty like a soldier storming a

wall.

278.

As we bear with children, so the

philosopher will bear with everybody.

279.

No one will ever persuade me that I

love my friends too much.

280.

Sextus taught me to bear with ignorant people,

and those who make up their minds without

examination.

281.

Fight fortune with thine own weapons, for she
will give thee none which can be used
against herself.

282.

No one can be despised by others, unless he
has first been despised by himself.

283.

Fear thyself more than any other witness of
thy sins, for thou art the only one thou canst
never escape.

284.

It is our minds that make us rich.

285.

It is better to get the start of a request
than to follow it.

286.

No one loves his country because she is great,
but because she is his own.

287.

The best proof that thy soul is calm is thy
ability to continue in thine own company.

288.

It is beautiful to yield to a law, to a ruler,
or to a wiser man.

289.

Profligacy loses basely what she must recover in ways still more base.

290.

Think of each day as in itself a life.

291.

He who is separate from any neighbor has fallen away from the whole community.

292.

The soul which is incapable of anger may be not feeble, but possessed of stronger impulses.

293.

There is nothing grand that is not also calm.

294.

Strength of mind can come in no other way

than by studying diligently and

observing nature.

295.

We make others better by bearing with them, and

worse by finding fault.

296.

Never can there be courage where there is

not peace.

297.

If you would have other people feel grateful
to you, you must not only help them, but
love them.

298.

There is no veil over a star.

299.

A man should stand upright, and not be
kept upright by others.

300.

Here is an invader that should be met on the
frontier.

301.

Let me be good-natured with my friends, and
mild and easy with my enemies.

302.

Such are the researches for which we are born,
that we should find all the time allotted us
short.

303.

Why should I care what happens, while my soul
is above it?

304.

Courage is careful to preserve itself, and
ready to endure what is evil in appearance
only.

305.

Shall not our knowledge that God is our maker, father, and guardian, free us from grief or fear?

306.

He has the longest of lives who suffers not time to be lost.

307.

I will lessen no ones liberty.

308.

Goodness consists mainly in wishing to become good.

309.

True pleasure can never cease, nor be turned

into pain.

310.

If unwilling to rise in the morning, say to

thyself, I awake to do the work of a man.

311.

No one is owner of anothers will.

312.

Let us inflict punishment without

anger, and because it is useful, not because

revenge is sweet.

313.

He who hurries to repay an obligation shows an unwillingness to remain under it - which is ingratitude.

314.

All men are plainly bound together.

315.

To pardon everybody is as cruel as to pardon nobody.

316.

The wise man will be glad to marry and have children, for he had rather not live at all than live alone.

317.

We all have leisure for what we wish to do.

318.

Trust in yourself, and believe that you are

walking in the right way.

319.

Canst thou wish anything worse than death to

thy enemy? Be at ease. He will die even if you

keep quiet.

320.

One day does more for the educated man than

the longest life for them untaught.

321.

Covetousness permits no gratitude.

322.

What you would be ashamed of feeling
under obligation for do not accept.

323.

There is no disgrace in having our opinions
change with the circumstances.

324.

Men exist for one another; therefore
teach them or bear with them.

325.

Care for other men and serve the common

brotherhood.

326.

Truth conquers by itself, opinion by

appealing to externals.

327.

The law aims to do men good, but this it

cannot accomplish unless they are

willing.

328.

Men are made for helping each other.

329.

So live as to have no secrets which you would not have known to your enemies.

330.

Despising death, welcoming poverty, and restraining lust, these three give great delight.

331.

What is given imprudently is lost culpably, and more so for doing no good than for making no return.

332.

A man cannot retain his wisdom, unless he has friends like himself.

333.

Love practically the men with whom thy lot is cast.

334.

What disgraces philosophy more than seeking applause?

335.

Look within: there is the fountain of good which will always gush forth, if thou wilt always dig.

336.

He who would be independent must seek for nothing and flee from nothing which depends on others.

337.

The wise man will pardon much, and save many souls because they are capable of being healed.

338.

Nothing comes upon any man which he is not formed to bear.

339.

Your excellence is your reason; adorn that and make it beautiful.

340.

We live for but a small part of the time, and the remaining part is not to be called life.

341.

Many would reach wisdom, did they not suppose they had already arrived there.

342.

He is poor who has need of others, and has not in himself all he wants.

343.

Nature endears man to man.

344.

Sin is never to be overcome by sin.

345.

To have kingdoms is fortune to give them,

virtue.

346.

Human life consists of kindness and harmony,

and is held together for mutual help, not by

terror, but by love.

347.

How much better worth our while to know what

we should do, than what has been already done!

348.

He is king who fears nothing and longs for

nothing. Everyone may give himself the

kingdom of noble thoughts.

349.

The safest road to virtue is repentance.

350.

The faith which expects rewards is to be

conquered by them.

351.

Love mankind.

352.

Do nothing but what is useful to men.

353.

The passions are as bad servants as leaders.

354.

Snow-white old age comes to the patient.

355.

Better leave crime unpunished than

condemn the innocent.

356.

He who knows that men are not born wise, but

have to become so, will never be angry with the

erring.

357.

Use the present thoughtfully and

justly, for life is short.

358.

That which is not good for the swarm is not

good for the bee.

359.

He who boasts his birth prides himself on what

belongs to others.

360.

Truth hates delay.

361.

Ease without letters is a living death and burial.

362.

We are created for the sake of mankind, to be useful to each other.

363.

As glory follows those who flee from her, so is gratitude given most richly to those who tolerate ingratitude.

364.

Money is the fools master, but the wise mans slave.

365.

Nothing is baser than to wish for death.

366.

This is education, to learn to wish that

things should happen as they do.

367.

Every soul is created to accept what is true,

reject what is false, and doubt what is

uncertain.

368.

The injury itself harms greatly the wrongdoer.

369.

Him who is provoked at you, attack with kindnesses, and his wrath will cease.

370.

We are made for cooperation, like the hands and feet.

371.

Nothing does more to strengthen the character in virtue, and free it from vice, than the society of the good.

372.

Time delivers fools from grief, and reason wise men.

373.

He who believes that we are all born of God
can never think of himself meanly or
basely.

374.

Do not think like him who wrongs thee, or as
he would have thee, but see what is required by
the truth.

375.

Freedom is not gained by satisfying, but by
restraining, our desires.

376.

He who lays out each day as if it were a life
will neither fear nor long for the morrow.

377.

Philosophy neither accepts nor rejects

any one, but shines for all.

378.

Thou art suffering justly; for thou

wishest to become good tomorrow, rather than

to be so today.

379.

In order not to be angry with anybody, you

should pardon everybody. Your

forgiveness is due to your race.

380.

A reasoning being goes on his way well, when

he directs his impulses only to actions of

public benefit.

381.

As soon as a child is born to us, it is no longer in our power not to love it and care for it.

382.

Great favors are often spoilt by being given slowly and sadly, and as if they were refused.

383.

What compulsion does, passes away, what persuasion does, endures.

384.

It is like a deserter to flee away from social laws.

385.

One universe is our common parent.

386.

Beware of feeling toward the cruel as they do toward others.

387.

Flatterers destroy the souls of men by blinding their eyes.

388.

Hunger needs little, but pride needs much.

389.

Neither self-respect nor prudence is shown by him who readily thinks himself despised.

390.

The first law of friendship is equality.

391.

Try to gather around your house, not herds of oxen, but troops of friends.

392.

The greatest waste of time is the delay which takes away our present, while promising a future.

393.

Virtue may be born in any place.

394.

Whoever shuns, or desires, what is not

in his own power, cannot be either

faithful or free.

395.

Nature, conscious of her own wisdom and beauty,

has created us as observers of lofty

spectacles.

396.

It is absurd to lose our own innocence rather

than to do harm to other people.

397.

So live among men as if God saw you. So speak

to God as if men heard you.

398.

They who do not keep striving to advance

fall back; no one finds his progress as he left

it.

399.

God gives man power never to let himself

be separated from the great whole.

400.

Prosperity gives friends; adversity

proves them.

If you enjoyed this

Stoic Cryptogram puzzle book,

please consider leaving

a review on Amazon.

Carpe Diem Publications